Married to Brazil

by
Alan Bachmann

with
Lee Carver

Dedication

You and I have one thing in common. We are spending our most precious commodity, the coin of life. Read with a mirror to see what God can and will do to lead you through the ups and downs of life. He can best spend the coin of your life. May the lines you read point you to the all forgiving God and not to the writer.

Acknowledgments

To God who loved us forgave and guided us, transforming our mere existence into the reason for being and gave us the noble privilege to serve as His ambassadors.

To Barbara, faithful wife, mother grand and great, matriarch of a legacy of lives, God given.

To Mrs. Lee Carver, a professional writer and author who lived in Brazil for a number of years, has worked incessantly to edit and put together an account of some episodes we lived and polished my English to be read and enjoyed.

Table of Contents

Chapter 1: THE AMAZON - OUR VILLAGE

Barbara and I took our first tenuous steps off the boat into a life full of more surprises than we could have imagined in our wildest dreams. We moved in 1960 to the exotic, mysterious Amazon. Our adventure was about to begin.

From the Atlantic Ocean we traveled to the mouth of the Amazon going north about the same distance as one would come south from Miami. The Amazon dumps so much fresh water into the ocean that 100 miles off the mouth of the Amazon, you may dip fresh water from the sea. By ship we navigated west 600 miles up the Amazon River. Just before reaching the city of Manaus, we turned left, to the south. We gazed upon the Madeira River, the "river of wood," about two to three miles wide where it joined the Amazon. It seemed muddier. Where they joined was notorious for sudden, violent storms. From there, we traveled five days upriver on a noisy boat.

Hammocks hung under the covered deck, a common practice on these riverboats that ran day and night up and down the river. Food was served at a long table with wooden benches on both sides. Getting a spot depended on how agile we were when the pots of food came out and porcelain tin plates were located with a metal spoon at each position. There was also a toilet bowl and a shower to the rear of the boat, both better not described. It was a way of life and travel for most river dwellers.

There was our destination, sitting high on a bluff! We arrived at the village where we were to begin our missionary career among the 1200 residents. When the river reached its highest level as rainy season ended, the Madeira River was still some thirty feet below despite rising more than thirty-five feet. Tree trunks came floating by with the current, thus the name "Wood River."

The village name, Manicoré, derived from the Guaraní language. The ambiguity could mean "food for" or "spirit of" a pig. We soon discovered that the people lived by a strange set of behaviorisms; a mix of the predominant religion, animism and spiritualist practices with a heavy dose of immorality. From the beginning, we encountered a strong resistance to the message of the gospel. During an earlier attempt, the missionaries had been burned in effigy (dolls looking like them) on a cross belonging to the existent religion. We knew immediately that the problem was one that has existed since creation: light hurt the eyes of those who lived in darkness!

The challenge: would God give us the gift of compassion to reach these people with the message of His salvation? We asked the

Lord to show us how to communicate His message to them. If they would not listen, we could say nothing to them, but we knew they would watch us closely.

Along the river bluff sat a line of a few row houses. We moved into one of them looking out over the river. What a view! Just beyond the sidewalk ten feet away was the edge of the river bluff. The river below stretched about a mile across to the other shore.

These houses were built by the Portuguese when they settled in the Amazon before the 1900's. Having no cement, they had built their very thick walls with a mix of lime, clay and rock. A clay tile roof with no intervening ceiling resulted in a constant battle for us to keep things dry. Every time a torrential rain came, it sprayed us and everything below.

We looked up at the clay tiles that made up the roof. A little sunlight or moonlight peeked through. Under the wooden floor there was an air space supposedly to reduce the moisture. The rotten wood needed to be replaced. When we removed the flooring, we found a huge assortment of ancient medicine bottles in all shapes and sizes that had been thrown there over many decades. A collector would have seen a fortune in them, but the bottles all went swimming.

As I poked around under the floor, I saw in the corner what looked like a tire. It was too thin to be a car tire and too thick for a motorcycle. Besides, this village had no vehicles. The thing was shiny, dark yellow, and had a uniform pattern of black blotches. It started moving. I had seen boa constrictors and anacondas, but this was something else.

I found a six-foot harpoon shaft made of iron wood. Carefully I rigged a rope to the end of the harpoon shaft, forming a noose. I prodded the snake until its head came into view. I slipped the noose over its head and pulled the rope very tight and dragged it out the door toward the drop-off at the river bluff.

An elderly gent from the congregation stopped by and asked what I was doing. "Do you know that your noose holds a deadly poisonous bushmaster?"

I held on tight while he went for an axe. The axe sent the head and its venom over the river bluff. This ten-foot bushmaster would never again endanger anyone. To think that it had lived right under our feet! It might just as well have come up into the house to have a look around.

With all the adjustments to this new world, we still looked forward to the day we could show compassion. The road of preparation that brought us to this moment was a long one. But how could we prepare for the unknown? We couldn't. But God knew every step before we took it, and we put our trust in Him.

If you want favor with both God and man, and a reputation for good judgment and common sense, then trust the Lord completely; don't ever trust yourself.

Proverbs 3:5(TLB)

Chapter 2: THE DREAM

It doesn't just happen. It's part of a process. But where does a dream begin? How and when does it become a reality? I got to thinking about this. I tried to put my finger on pieces that puzzled me. The components probably began somewhere in adolescence. Certainly I was not aware of what God was preparing for me, and at the time I had not the least bit of interest in being a missionary. I did have godly parents.

By age ten, my first summer job was for a hard working Italian immigrant at his truck farm weeding strawberry plants and crawling along on my hands and knees. I didn't last long, but I learned a lot.

Next I took on any odd job in our town of East Brookfield, MA. I mowed lawns, raked leaves, shoveled snow, whatever job was available. I landed an after-school job at Varney's Variety store restocking shelves and taking out the trash. In the winter, I chopped blocks of ice from the lake for his soda pop coolers. We skated on the frozen water and summers, swam in it. As spring came, I painted his rowboats, put them in the water and prepared canoes and boats for rental.

On weekends or holidays, my dad always had a project going around home. Dad, an air conditioning engineer with Carrier, was always making improvements. I helped him and learned to build with lumber, work with concrete, masonry, painting, plumbing, and jobs of all sorts.

The nearby town of West Brookfield had a General Store. The proprietor was a Mr. Allan Wheeler. One stop shopping for farmers and town's people, the store sold clothes, shoes, all sorts of hunting and fishing needs, molasses pumped from a barrel, meats, fish, you name it. Neither West or East Brookfield had a high school. Both towns had daily bus runs to take their students to a regional high school. There I met Barbara Wheeler, and eventually would ask her dad for her hand in marriage.

During high school I set out to build a "Hot Rod." I spent long

nights in our two-car garage. Money mattered, so I picked up what I could at the junk yard. My brother Robert pitched in, and I ended up with a '39 Ford V-8 coupe with eight exhaust pipes, four on each side of the engine going into two collector mufflers. No sooner was it up and running than I lost interest and sensed it would not be part of my future.

A new look at life came when I saw myself as a rebel. A sinner, incapable of doing anything to change my set of values. God stepped into my life, forgave me, and transformed me to want to please Him in what I was and what I would do.

Summer vacations during high school, I worked in New Jersey on a sport fishing yacht. I learned a lot about lines, engines and navigation. Every day started at 6:00, getting ready to go to sea. The yacht was harbored at Barnegat Light on Long Beach Island, six miles at sea by a causeway. Barbara and I had just graduated from a Regional High School in Spencer, Massachusetts. I had been class president and Barbara, yearbook editor. She was on the island for the

first time and got a job working at Harvey Cedars Bible Conference. When I came in from offshore, I cleaned up the yacht and went most nights to the meetings. Oh, of course, Barbara and I sat together. It was there that God spoke to us about the coin of life. We had already enrolled in Northeastern Bible College in New Jersey. Looking ahead, we felt firmly that we now knew the direction our lives would take. But we were yet to know what and how it all would get us there.

At Northeastern, Barbara was assistant cook. I worked in maintenance at the school and pumped gas part time. I even studied some. I learned to fly, but with all the water in Brazil, I could get around by boat. Flying was for those specially prepared, not an option for me on the mission field.

While at Northeastern Bible College, Barbara and I could see the example of serious Christianity in the staff and teachers. We served in a local church on weekends.

We were asked to begin a junior high group. Later we worked with the high schoolers and later with the college students. By the end of Northeastern we had learned a bit about ourselves and about people.

Saturday, we both graduated from Northeastern with plans to be off Monday to linguistic studies in Oklahoma and on to California for a course in Missionary Medicine and Dentistry. The day before, all this was still a dream. Our plans were based on full blown faith. We had no bank account nor did we know how to write a check. Plastic money hadn't been invented. On Saturday we had no gas, no cash.

Graduation that afternoon was in open air on the athletic field where a large platform had been set up in the center of the field. We students had set up rows and rows of chairs. On this beautiful June day, the chairs were full as the graduating class marched in caps and gowns toward the platform. The school song and all the speeches became a blur.

As we marched from the platform, I could now see the faces of those who came. I recognized several from the church where Barbara and I served those three years with the youth. Some of these same people were present when we were married in the chapel by our pastor, who was also president of Northeastern.

Not only did the pastor entrust us with responsibility for the youth, but quite a few of the six hundred members of the church were praying for us. Some ventured to encourage us in a specific way concerning what they saw our gifting to be.

Few knew of our hopes. We hadn't told many at church of our dream, but the word circulated. Unknown to us, many of them were praying us on our way. God gave us the funds through ways we could not imagine. After the ceremony and hugs from Mom and Dad, folks from church and a few others stayed around to wish us well. Cards and more cards were handed to us.

We later discovered each card contained a gift in cash. This we could never have imagined!

Monday we stuffed ourselves and what would fit in our little car and rode off into a future as bright as God's promises. After an intense linguistic course in Oklahoma, we arrived in Los Angeles and settled into a little cottage. We bought a box of cereal, a loaf of bread, a bottle of milk, and with nineteen cents and a tank of gasoline, we began the next step of faith as we enrolled in the course of missionary medicine in downtown LA at Biola.

The most important piece of baggage that went with us from Northeastern and onward was the Godly example of those who were giving of their lives to start us on the same life of faith we could see in those around us.

And it is he who will supply all your needs
from his riches in glory
because of what Christ Jesus has done for us.

Philippians 4:19(TLB)

Chapter 3: THE DREAM GROWS FEET

We wanted to spend the coin of our lives serving God in a remote region of the world. Following studies in the Bible and linguistics, Barbara and I enrolled in BIOLA School of Missionary Medicine. Classes were taught by leading physicians, many with experience in foreign lands. We were eighteen students with a selection of twenty-one medical doctors. In Los Angeles we trained in three hospitals, in obstetrics, nursery all the way to geriatrics. We were awaiting our first baby Beth, born in the obstetrics department where Barbara had worked. After final exams, Hollywood Presbyterian Hospital asked me to work in the surgical unit as an orderly. I stayed on two months. Twenty or more surgeries were scheduled daily. When not bringing or removing a patient, I could observe some procedures performed by top-notch surgeons.

Two things soon occurred. The nurses learned that Barbara and I were headed for some remote region of the Amazon. They knew I was trying to learn the basics of medical care. As soon as the surgery ended, the suite had to be cleaned and set up for the next surgery. The ends of rolls of adhesive tape, trays with needles, suture material, ampoules of medications, all had to be cleared out. There was no time to sort out the sutures and other items to return them to their jars or storage. Adhesive tape rolls of various widths were refilled. Whatever might be left unused on the tray had to be removed. The nurses set aside a large plastic barrel labeled in large letters, "FOR ALAN."

The barrel began to fill with partial rolls of adhesive tape, ampoules, sutures, and other materials. By this time I was practicing all types of suturing on the gurney blankets, using instruments, until I could stitch them rapidly and do the various ties.

On occasion one of the surgeons would call me in to observe a certain procedure. "You might have to do this some time back in the jungle." *(And who's dreaming now?)* But I listened and watched. I felt like I was filming it in my head.

The blur of classes and shifts in the hospital easily dulled my perspective. I worked to keep my focus. A book, *The Burma Surgeon*, caught my eye. Doctor Seagraves spent his life in the hills of Burma (Myanmar) during the Second World War. He trained girls of the Karen Tribe. They became known as the best nurses during the war years. Later I met a radio producer in Singapore, originally from Burma, who told me of the fame of these Karen tribal girls as nurses.

Dr. Seagraves' biography, *The Burma Surgeon*, set me to dream with my eyes wide open. Could I care for those who would otherwise have no help? Could I? A dream list began—surgical instruments, dental forceps and such, essential for performing medical and dental procedures in the Amazon.

The steps of good men are directed by the Lord. He delights in each step they take.

Psalm 37:23(TLB)

Chapter 4: SHOES FOR THE DREAM'S FEET

I stepped through the door of a physicians' equipment exchange in Los Angeles, anxious to test the reality of this list of surgical and dental instruments I hoped to take to the Amazon. We had saved a jar full of pennies to put shoes on my dream feet and buy a few things. Innocent me!

The shop owner looked at the list. He looked at me. "If you don't have a Physician's license, just forget it."

I couldn't hide my disappointment.

His expression challenged me and my right to place such an order. "And what do you think you would do with these surgical and dental instruments?"

"My wife and I are preparing to go to the Amazon jungles." I began to tell him my dream. "We will be five to seven days upriver from any medical resource. I may need to attend to any emergency that happens."

Clyde's mood changed so much that I could not imagine what his next remark might be.

His face flushed, and his eyes moistened. He swallowed hard. "When I flew airplanes over the Pacific islands, I could see little villages of natives. I often wondered, will anyone find these people, learn their language and tell them about God's son?" Obviously he was a follower of Christ and had been so during his military career.

Clyde looked up and with a smile said, "Certainly none of this which you hope to acquire will be used in the USA."

I assured him that it would only be used in that remote region of the Amazon.

"Take your jar of pennies with you and come back in a week. Don´t bring the penny jar."

Hard at work in the surgical unit of Hollywood Presbyterian Hospital, I could hardly wait until the moment when I would return to the Physician's Exchange. When I walked in Clyde met me with a big smile. He began to place on the counter all kinds of instruments which I recognized. I became excited to see dental forceps and accessory tools. In my mind I began naming the surgical instruments as he laid them on the counter. Was I dreaming? Would they be a part of my resources?

Clyde looked like a kid with his favorite toys.

"Look Clyde, this would be great, but I can't handle the cost of all this."

"And who said I would let you pay?" He went on to talk about what we hoped to do as if he himself were going with us. "For years I wondered how I could do something like this."

Who could place a monetary value on all that Clyde gave? No, he gave from his heart. It was given for the work of the Lord under our care in the Amazon.

For whoever finds me finds life
and wins approval from the Lord.

Proverbs 8:35 (TLB)

Chapter 5: THE INVISIBLE BRIDGE

"Gramps, if you and Grams came to Brazil by ship that took weeks way back then, why do you talk about a bridge? Do you have a picture of this bridge?"

"This bridge is real, but you can't see it. Between any two culture worlds a big change should take place in your attitude and how you think. I call it a bridge, because it connects you from one culture and language to the other. The idea is to leave most of your cultural baggage on one side of this crossover bridge and pick up the culture you are stepping into. You kids grew up in Brazil, so how you think and speak is all very natural to you.

"When Grams and I arrived as youngsters, we brought baggage with the ship. No problem. But we had cultural baggage in our heads that needed to be checked out.

"And that makes me think of walking across a bridge. The less culture we carried in our heads, the easier the job of crossing over the culture and language bridge would be. Grams and I had to be ready to make a trade. If we held on to the culture of our origin, we would resist trying to see life through Brazilian eyes. We would have a real struggle to learn to think like a Brazilian."

"Gramps, when you left North America did you think about this?"

"No, not then, but when we arrived here we began to learn that this is a different world from the one in which we grew up. We thought a lot about this. Could we become part of Brazilian society which is so natural for you and your moms and dads? You were born here.

"Grams and I faced real tensions. If we attempted to hold on to or defend patriotic sentiment from the other side of this bridge, we would miss the purpose of coming."

"What do you mean?"

"We did not to come to Brazil to represent our homeland. It's fine for people from any country in the world to come to Brazil and be known for the country they are from. We came for a different purpose. That's why you are Brazilians. Your moms and dads grew up here."

"Gramps, why did you and Grams try so hard to be like Brazilians?"

"Look at it this way. An ambassador represents the one who sent him. Grams and I came to Brazil to represent the Lord Jesus as best we could. When Brazilians hear what we say and watch what we do, Grams and I have always hoped they will identify us with the Lord Jesus. The attempt to identify with Brazil's language and culture is hard work and for us that goes on forever.

"Does everybody feel this way, Gramps?"

"Kids, for some people the cross-over is so traumatic to let go of cultural ties that they never make it across this culture bridge. Arriving in Brazil, we soon had a first impression of what 'crossing the bridge' would mean to us.

"So, what came off the culture bridge? We hoped we had left a lot on the other side! Here's how it went.

"Brazilian friends came into our lives ready to observe and guide us to understand Brazilian ways of thinking and doing. They gave very helpful advice, were patient and sympathetic. Many contrasts stared us in the face, the differences between here and "back home" were rough! Anytime we tried to compare Brazilian culture with the other side of the bridge we often ended up with a contrast."

"What was Brazil like when you and Grams came?"

"The Brazil you grandkids never saw was different from today, at least as it looked to us. What was Brazil like 50 years ago? Men's shirts were very form fitting, including the sleeves. Trousers were tailored well and looked pretty classy. Shoes, of real leather, were the best. In those days most clothing was sewn by a tailor or seamstress. Women's clothing was designed by women and was extremely modest, always worn with a petticoat or half slip. Clothes were made to order according to the wearer's request and done on simple sewing machines. Today globalization dominates a lot of areas of life. The world has become a global village.

"In those days, we learned much through our language classes. Grams made acquaintance with a girl who lived nearby. Altamira was an executive secretary. Afternoons she came along the sidewalk with a niece in hand. Then, no young Brazilian girl left the house alone since it easily could give the wrong message. After a while, she stopped at our wooden gate at the house where we lived while in language school. Our daughter Beth and the little niece were soon friends. Grams and Altamira too. Altamira began taking Grams to the open market to shop, to the hair dresser's, to the dressmaker's, anywhere and everywhere. Altamira became a shadow for Grams and would haggle over prices and purchases. Although Grams was not yet able do this, she was 'learning the ropes' from her friend.

"Mornings I rode two buses across town to the language course. On the bus, I met a very fine law student named Mario. When he understood that I wanted to know the Brazilian mind-set and the how and why of things, he latched onto me with all of his enthusiasm. It was obvious that I would learn a great deal, if I did not disagree with things he told me or showed me. I could see so many points in contrast with culture on the other side of the bridge. He knew what he was saying. I had to learn.

"Objectivity would be our key to learning. Any comparisons with life and practice on the other side of the culture bridge would bring no help. I boarded the bus one morning wearing leather sandals and socks. Mario looked at me visibly shaken. 'What are you doing going to school with a fever? And to top it all, you shaved!' The presence of socks while using sandals suggested you had a fever, in which case you would also remain unshaven.

"Hand gestures were part of my talking. If Mario saw me using a gesture from the 'other side of the bridge,' or one that was not decent or meant something different, he would quickly warn me. If the meaning of the gesture in Brazilian culture was bad, he would tell me why I could not use that gesture. Did I learn fast!

"Business people wore white linen suits with a plain black tie. If there had been a recent death in the family, the man would wear a black strip of cloth pinned to his top jacket pocket or on the pocket of his shirt. Women might dress in black for a specific time of mourning.

"It became clear to Grams and me that the less cultural baggage we came off the bridge with, the easier it became to assimilate Brazilian culture. That unseen bridge between cultures and languages was cluttered with traps that could wreck a person. Grams and I were young and radical. There used to be a phrase in English which said 'go for broke' which for Grams and I meant 'do or die trying.' Total commitment is easier said than done. That attitude helped us to cross over successfully. Some never make it. Too much baggage comes over the bridge because they don't let go!

"And one certainly must cross the culture bridge.

"The ambassadorial charge to represent our Lord needs to be as free as possible of cultural trappings from the other side of the bridge. The Biblical message of salvation must transcend cultural 'spins' that could be misconstrued as a religious importation.

"Time taught us some tricks. When later I studied for entrance exams to a Brazilian University, political challenges to American politics quickly ceased when I responded, 'Hey, I was born there, but go find somebody who knows about American politics and ask them.' The implication was that I was a political ignoramus. Friendships developed with many. They sensed I was more eager to listen to them extol their culture and outlook than to discuss the culture I came from.

"When you grandkids were growing up, Gramps traveled to some of the twenty-three countries of Latin America to train radio producers. Spanish is a beautiful language easy to learn after our Portuguese. The reverse way, from Spanish to Portuguese, can take forever. We understand Spanish but they don't understand our Portuguese. I loved speaking Spanish and used it constantly for about ten years. Often I was asked my name. I replied with German sounding, "Bachmann."

"They would exclaim with approval '*Aleman, si?*' (German, yes?)

"'How did you guess?' I would ask. They preferred to see me as a German. This ended the question of roots. If you don't make a case of it, others won't."

Yes, whatever a person is like, I try to find common ground with him so that he will let me tell him about Christ and let Christ save him.

Corinthians 9:22 (TLB)

Chapter 6: THE VILLAGE DENTIST

Were we ready for a surprise? Would we show compassion as we hoped? That day came, but not the way we thought.

My wife Barbara got me in "hot water" (more than once). She was talking with our neighbor lady, out front on the walk way which stretched along in front of these ancient row-houses. The neighbor lady and Barbara hoped to catch any breeze as they looked out over our majestic Madeira River. She was telling Barbara about her little girl suffering with a very bad toothache. She explained to Barbara that she would have to go downriver to Manaus, the capital city of the Amazon. The riverboat, going with the current, would still take at least four days. In the big city the lady would then need to find some place to stay. After going to the dentist, the return upriver would be longer, another six days on a riverboat that carried passengers navigating against the strong river currents.

When Barbara heard the neighbor lady explain all this, she said: "Well, my husband knows how to extract teeth. He can give the anesthetic and remove your child's tooth." Frankly, I was not very excited about Barbara's offer to enlist my services to be a Dentist.

I prepared my instruments and the mother brought her little girl to me. Once I had applied a local anesthetic, I then proceeded to extract the tooth with no complications. This was our first experience to serve people in this way. When I took a course in missionary dentistry before coming to Brazil, I believed that this skill would be just enough to take care of my own family so distant from professional help. But God planned things differently. He chose to use this gift to show people He loved them through us. Little did we know that helping this little girl would be the beginning of many adventures as a dentist.

The sun gets an early start in the jungle and brings plenty of steamy heat with it. We had just finished eating our banana porridge for breakfast. About 7:00, we heard someone clapping at the door. Clapping announces the person where doorbells and electricity do not exist. When I opened the door, to my surprise, some twenty people were standing in the yard.

Each person wanted a "few" teeth extracted! That one little girl's tooth extraction made the rounds by the "jungle vine radio." Word of mouth spreads fast. Thus began the saga that turned me into a missionary dentist. This river village, like any in those days, found only the desperate or very courageous who would allow someone to extract a tooth using a pair of scissors or pliers, with no anesthesia and no hygiene.

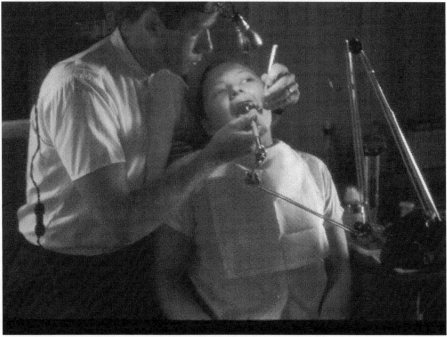

Alan Bachmann

We preach more messages with our lives than with our voices.

In everything set them an example by doing what is good. In your teaching show integrity, seriousness.

Titus 2:7 (NIV)

Chapter 7: THE CRIPPLE WHO WASN'T

We were not really accustomed to life in the village when a man in the congregation asked me along in his little riverboat. He wanted to evangelize. He was unsure of himself and asked me to go along. We headed downriver from Manicoré. After an hour or so, we turned off this coffee-colored muddy Madeira River into a "black coffee" that poured out of the Atininga River. This river runs somewhat parallel to the Madeira River from its source far back in the jungle. By nightfall, John and I had chugged some distance upriver in his little boat.

We came to a group of houses where we hoped to tie up for the night. The launch was too small to fit even one hammock on board and we did not want to be a free meal for the malarial mosquito through the night. We ventured a "hallo the house."

"*Come on up.*" From the top of a wooden log ladder, a young fellow invited us. The stilts of the house, about seven feet high, served several purposes. There was space to shelter pigs, chickens and whatever under the house. Building it the extra height resulted from experience when the river rose too high. And at that height the mosquito population was not so strong.

As we reached the top of the ladder, we first saw what had once been rough-hewn boards, now polished smooth with season after season of husking corn, beans and anything else to be done covered from the rain and as time permitted in the evening sitting on the floor. As we rose higher on the ladder, I saw a man to my left who seemed to be squatting in an unusual manner. As I could observe in the course of our visit, this man, Jacob, was very crippled. His squat was about his only position.

The evening wore on and as was the custom, the visitor brought news, traded comments, and generally conversed with the family. It finally came out that I was a Pastor, and one people insisted was also a doctor. It ended up that I consulted with various ones as to their ailments and symptoms.

Then "Cripple Jake," as he was known to everyone, asked me if I could "cure" him. That put me on the spot. I listened intently to his story as he embellished it beyond what I was seeing. I frankly do not recall saying anything significant except to share with him my faith in a living, loving Savior who had forgiven me of my sin. I did give him an injection and left another and recommended medication he could find in Manicoré where I lived. The evening was very long. At dawn we were on our way.

I'm not sure of the time span, but probably some months had passed when one day a young fellow was brought to me who had been bitten by a snake. He knew it was deadly. Without the right serum he would be dead in a very short time with the onset of respiratory paralysis or hemorrhaging, depending on the type of snake. He hoped I would have an anecdote of the right kind of serum in our kerosene refrigerator. I injected it as therapy indicated. Then we waited.

I asked the young fellow where he lived and where he had been bitten by the snake. He said he was from the Atininga River.

"Did you live anywhere near 'Cripple Jake?'"

"Yes, I know him. He has the name, but now he walks around just like anybody," he answered emphatically.

If his information was accurate—and there seemed no reason to fabricate it, for he did not know anything about my visit in the house on stilts of "Cripple Jake"—certainly Jake had experienced the "Touch of the Master's Hand."

O Lord, the poor man trusts himself to you; you are known as the helper of the helpless.

Psalm 10:14b (TLB)

Chapter 8: NO, NOT FROM HORNETS

Nelson and I were in water up to our necks with our backs against the stern of the river launch. The keel was dragging in the mud of the lake bottom, now shallow in the dry season. How did we get in to this predicament?

We had run two days upriver from our village to take two linguistic scientists to a river that flows into this lake at the Parintintin tribe. Nelson and I off-loaded their basic supplies and left the missionaries there. Their calling was an assignment which would take a number of years. They were reducing the spoken language to a written form using symbols of an international alphabet that could be read by other linguists. The natives would have the Bible translated into their language .Our part was to be a supply line to these ladies. On board we had loaded their supplies: a sack of rice, tins of kerosene for their Aladdin Lamp, sugar, salt, bars of laundry soap, and such. They had the basics to enable them to live for many months in their palm house in the tribe and perform this demanding task.

Chugging upriver I experienced no unexpected circumstances. We navigated well around the shallows and kept clear of strong swirling currents, rocks, and stumps. Late on the second day, we entered and crossed Great Snail Lake. I would later live on this lake with my family. We came to the Ipixuna River that poured its flow into this lake at the end of its long journey from far back in the jungle. A short distance up the river we came to the little house where we would offload the supplies and say goodbye to the linguist missionaries.

In travel to this tribal village, the supplies had been stacked on the bow of the boat. The bow would now ride higher in the water while at the same time the stern or back end of the launch would ride lower in the water. The Indians always asked for our used crankcase oil from the motor, which I kept in liter bottles. They slicked it on their straight black hair and it really added a shine. With their bow and arrows, they speared a couple of big bass—I never saw an Indian miss—so we could eat. By nightfall we were on our way down the river into the lake to cross it. We would then go on out through the connecting waterway into the mighty Madeira River.

As we crossed the lake, which was at its lowest level of the year, the keel of the river launch began dragging in the mud on the bottom of the lake. Since unloading all of the supplies that were in the forward part of the launch, we were now down some in the stern. The keel protects the launch's bottom and planking. It extends downward at a slant and ends just beyond the propeller where the rudder is. If I added power, the stern would sit lower.

What to do? The solution was to turn off the engine and get in the water and push the boat from behind until we reached deeper water near the outflow of the lake. The mud was soft. To keep from sinking in as we pushed, we took two short floor boards from alongside the diesel engine and put them down on the lake bottom to step on so we could push and not sink into the mud.

You guessed it. Every time we moved the boat forward a bit, we had to go under water and pull out of the mud the boards we had been standing on. We then reset them closer to the stern that distance we had advanced with our pushing. It was exhausting work. After a while, we placed the two boards up on the stern and climbed on board and made some coffee. We sat on the bow of the launch for a brief rest and to catch whatever breeze we could. We were exhausted from pushing the launch which was dragging its keel on the lake bottom.

Nelson picked up our spotlight, turned it on, and began to shine it ahead to where we hoped to push the launch into deeper water. We sat dumfounded as we saw hundreds of eyes caught in the spotlight. They belonged to this multitude of alligators all around us! With the lake being thirty to thirty-five feet below its high water level, all of the alligators were forced to congregate in the lake until the jungles flooded again in the coming rainy season. Well, they hadn't bothered us so far! We certainly hoped we wouldn't find out just how hungry these "gators" might be.

Back in the water with our floor boards, we continued to push with renewed effort and finally reached deeper water, enough to dive in and rescue our floor boards. We cranked up the noisy diesel engine with its straight exhaust pipe, breaking the silence of the jungle night. Now we were homeward bound going out the waterway and down the Madeira River.

We waived goodbye to those hungry 'gator eyes and left them to find a meal where we wouldn't be part of the menu.

When I moved to the lake with my family, we occasionally would have a gator in for a meal. Not as a guest, but the main course.

Nelson? How did I first meet him? I guess I could give Nelson the new name "Onesimus" after the one St. Paul talks about in the Letter to Philemon. Likewise Nelson went from "useless" to "useful," as demonstrated during that river trip.

My first encounter with Nelson was seeing him in the congregation of the little church high above the river in our village. As I preached, I noticed him slip into church and sit on a bench in the back. My recollection of that evening was that it seemed as if I were hearing a loud whisper coming from the jungle outside the church. I later learned that I was not imagining things.

The following morning after that church service, I went down to the river to get an eighteen liter can of water. By placing the five gallon kerosene can on my head with a gourd dipper floating on the water, I could make it up the river bank without spilling a drop. Nelson was already there when I arrived to dip my can in the river.

I greeted him and he replied without turning to look at me. This was very out of culture. When he did turn, his face looked like he had gotten into a hornet's nest.

"Nelson, what happened to you? Hornets?"

He told me how his brother was calling from the jungle the whole time he had listened to my sermon. When Nelson returned to their humble palm house, his brother beat him and threatened Nelson to never again listen to that follower of Jesus. He had not been injured from hornets as I first thought, but by the fists of his brother.

The social pressure to conform to the family was almost unbearable. However, Nelson replied, "I know that Jesus Christ can change my life. I will follow Him no matter what." And he did.

Nelson stuck with that decision. We enjoyed some other adventures together. A few years later, he moved to Amazon's Capital city of Manaus to further his studies. He remained faithful to the Lord.

Nelson's face healed, but more than that, he was now a "new creation" with his faith in the living Savior.

Then he said to all, "Anyone who wants to follow me must put aside his own desires and conveniences and carry his cross with him every day and keep close to me!

Luke 9:23 (TLB)

Chapter 9: NOT QUITE DEAD

How many times have I been called out of a comfortable night's sleep in my hammock? Illness and emergencies know no hour. When this call came, it was unusual.

"Doctor, come quick, Senhor Jamborangi just died!" I thought of my dear grandfather, Dr. William Bachmann, a general practitioner until his death at ninety-one years of age. At a call like this, he would have told the ones appealing for his presence to go "buy a coffin." His Germanic mentality was so very practical.

To console the family and show that I cared, I went to the modest little palm-covered board frame house to "pay my respects." In the corridor from the front door, the first room to the left had some wooden benches where people could sit. The next room going on to the hard packed clay floor which was the kitchen, there was a room with a little wooden bed and its straw mattress. There he was, stretched out, so to say, poor Jamborangi.

There was a great deal of commotion in the kitchen. Padre Ricardo, the local priest was there. Everybody was talking at once. "A coffin has to be made. Get him buried quickly."

I went right to the bedside by Jamborangi and kneeled down there by this dear man's body. I grabbed his hand as naturally as I would any sick person's. He was warm to the touch.

Believing that the last faculty to go is the hearing, I said to him, "If you hear me, blink three times." His eyes were closed, but he distinctly made the gesture three times.

Can one imagine this man still alive and hearing people planning to bury him? In the jungle, a body does not stay long out of the ground. Someone came into the room to light the candles, one on each of the four bedposts, to light his way in death. What a surprise to see me talking to a "dead" person.

I came back home straight away to begin therapy with medication that might reverse the stroke he had suffered. The quicker the medication could be administered, the more chance of reversing some of the effects.

A week or more went by, and who should come limping along the walk in front of the row houses? Yes, Jamborangi. He asked me for a New Testament. Knowing he could read and that his eyesight was not the best, I did have a large print New Testament. He proudly carried it home, limping along with great effort.

Did Jamborangi go on to heaven or not? It's not a question of any one religion, but to know the authority of the words of Jesus' promise. These same words are on the Tombstone of America's first president, George Washington:

"I am the resurrection and the life. Whoever believes in me, though he dies, yet shall he live! And whoever believes in me shall never die."

The words of Jesus in John 11:25

Chapter 10: NO SPIDERS, NO SHOES, NO FISH

NOT FOR BABIES

Titus, a humble river carrier, a stevedore, earned his living carrying heavy sacks and boxes up the steep steps from our river port.

It was around midnight. I heard clapping and rapping on our wooden door. I climbed out of my hammock, lifted the mosquito net, lit a *lamparina* and rather sleepily made it to the door. Titus was holding a *lamparina* and the shadow it cast over his face awoke me very quickly. "Titus, what's the matter?"

Titus answered: "Please come quickly. My baby daughter is thrashing around and screaming." *Convulsions? Fever?* Off we went over the trail to his home. I took a flashlight and a couple of things in a basket and walked along following him, pushing my bicycle.

We arrived at a typical jungle home of thatched palm. The entrance is a corridor which passes the front room where there might be a bench or two in order to receive a visit. To the right along this corridor was the room where all the hammocks are hung with their mosquito nets. It was hot and stuffy.

The mother was making every attempt to quiet the little baby who was screaming and wailing inconsolably. To no avail could the mother calm the baby. I did a quick check of the child and asked the mother several questions trying to get a history of the onset of this illness.

"What medication did you give the baby?"

"Uh, nothing!" she replied.

I quickly decided to pedal home over the twisting jungle trail as fast as I could, and return with a powerful injection which might help with these violent convulsions.

As I returned and neared the house, there was the most anguishing wail from the mother. Dropping the bike, I rushed into the house and found the baby dead in her arms.

As I entered along the narrow corridor I passed by a little shelf suspended from the palm thatch by strings. On it were scissors, needle and some thread, and then my flashlight fell on what looked like a bottle or two that might contain medicine. I again asked the mother, "What was the medicine you gave the baby?"

The first time I asked she had told me "*Nothing*." Now she said that she had given a little medicine from a very small bottle. She described the bottle and I located it on the shelf.

As I read the label by flashlight I asked the mother, "How much of it did you give your baby?"

"Just a little demitasse coffee spoonful."

"And why did you give it to the baby?"

She replied, "My neighbor told me it was good for spider bites."

The label on the bottle in question read: Tincture of Arsenic.

Spider bites? Maybe. Babies, no!

I destroyed the bottle and never said a word to either Titus or his wife. To raise questions of blame would destroy both parents and not bring the baby back. The mother would live with such remorse and Titus would not be able to forgive her. This was without thinking of repercussions with the neighbor.

NO MORE SHOES

I was outfitted in my cloth cap and molded rubber shoes made from the gum of the rubber tree, ready to travel on the river in my dugout canoe. My mosquito net, hammock, and clothes were stuffed in a rubber-coated grain sack, another creation made with rubber milk.

The sack was tied really tight. If I ran into rain or the canoe tipped over, nothing would get wet. The sack could also be used as a life preserver to help me swim to shore. I slung the sack over a canoe paddle on my shoulder, hobo-style. I was just about to climb down the earth steps cut in the river bluff to reach my canoe.

The shoemaker's wife called to me, "Oh doctor, please go see my husband. He is really bad off." Her husband was the town shoemaker. By the time it would take me to explain about my intended trip, I could go see her husband and then be on my way. What's a half hour delay when you're going somewhere by canoe?

So I examined our shoemaker and listened to his heart, lungs and poked about a bit. My diagnosis was that he had a massive infestation of intestinal parasitic worms migrating to his lungs. His was the most common of five types of intestinal parasites typically found in our people. So severe was the infestation that the worms migrating into his lungs could drown him. What a sound they made through my stethoscope!

In an oral based culture, people have superb memories since many can't write anything down. Their son confirmed that the medicine I prescribed was available. I also left the prescription written out in block letters with dosage details. I had done everything I could do, so again I started for the river bluff to my dugout canoe and paddled away.

Some four days later I returned to our little town. It wasn't long before I came across the shoemaker's wife, as drab as ever.

"How's your husband doing? Did you give the medicine I prescribed for him?"

"No, we didn't give him the medicine the way you told us to give it." She replied with her usual dismal demeanor.

Getting information from this lady was like pulling teeth. "Well, did you give him less or too much?"

"No, we decided to do nothing, and so we didn't give him any medicine. We were so afraid. He was terribly bad off."

"And how is your husband doing now?"

"We buried him yesterday," she replied stoically.

This shoemaker would make shoes no more.

DECISION DETERMINES DESTINY

It has been said, "The road to destruction is paved with good
    intentions."

Some decide to do nothing. That, too, is a decision.

Some decide on the basis of other people's guess work.

Few decide based on accurate information.

It's as true in life as it is for eternity. One way!

There is a way that seems right to man,
but the end of it is death.

King Solomon, in Proverbs 14:12

"FEED HIM TO THE FISH!"

The "Flying Boat," as the Catalina airplane was called, was a
faithful hold-over from the days of the Second World War, almost as
well known as the DC-3 which still flew in some places in the world.
In those days it was a common sight in the Amazon. The Catalina
came by once a week and landed out on the river. As it drifted down
with the current, a large freight canoe paddled out to tie up along the
side of the plane.

Two or three passengers stepped out of the plane's side door into
the canoe. Then several who were travelling got into the plane.
Baggage was exchanged in the same way. I was along in the canoe to
say goodbye to Barbara, flying to the city of Manaus. It was 9 AM and

already the sweltering heat was barely diminished by a breeze on the river. The pilot usually climbed out of the cabin through the window and sat on the upturned wheel in the shadow of the wing.

In the canoe with us was the Federal Tax Collector, infamous for his radical behavior, often under the influence of cane liquor. Known for being an expert shot, he could hit ducks on the wing with a rifle. He always carried a hand gun. There in the canoe, with no provocation, he turned on me with some very vitriolic language. I prayed silently that I would not add to this deplorable behavior by reacting to his remarks. The man was evidently drunk even this early in the day.

The pilot, sitting on the up-folded tire under the wing, saw the whole drama untold. "Feed him to the fish! Paste him a real good one and over he goes."

Had I done so, the tax collector probably would have drowned or been selected for a meal by the giant catfish found in the deep. Thus, the code of the jungle.

I prayed for God to keep me quiet, and soon we were loosed from the Catalina, and the canoe headed for shore. Climbing out of the canoe, the tax collector was very unsteady and probably would not have made it up the slippery clay steps to the port. I helped him against his strong protests. It was not the kind of experience that brings any satisfaction. One does what is right not because of how one feels.

The next day I was in the store of a friend, an Arab merchant known locally as "Old Farid." His father had probably come to Brazil to work on the Devil's Railroad. As I was selecting some antibiotics, worm medicine and other medications, who steps into the store? Yes, the tax collector, and perfectly sober! I dreaded what might happen next.

"I want everybody to know that this man is a man of God and nobody is going to harm him or they answer to me." He patted his gun to reinforce his declaration. He went on to say, "After the way I treated him in the canoe and how he then helped me…People don't do this. But this man did."

At the time of this incident, there were many overt comments against the pastor and his people. For whatever reason, God put this man into place as a protector. I didn't ask for this, but it ended a wave of threats against us. We became friends after a fashion, and once a month or so he butchered a cow in a local shed, and I was always able to buy a halfway decent piece of meat from his chop of the machete.

He grants good sense to the godly—his saints. He is their shield, protecting them and guarding their pathway.

Proverbs 2:8 (TLB)

Chapter 11: TWO WAYS TO PREACH

He came alongside our launch, where we were tied up at the river's edge of a large plantation. When he glided alongside, I was sitting on the bow next to the wheel. The spokes we held onto as we steered appeared to be in the shape of a particular red pepper, "malgueta," the nickname by which the wheel was called. This wheel was connected to the rudder by a system of chains to the stern of the launch behind the propeller. Holding onto this chain, "Mr. Canoe" had a request. "Could the doctor come with me to look at some folk in my village?"

Canoe paddle in his left hand, his right hand holding onto our launch against the river's current. I looked at this small man and his dug-out canoe. Simple, unadorned were the words he spoke, but there was strength of conviction in his voice. His clothes told me much. They were of the typical cloth that someone would have sewn by hand. Not even a pedal sewing machine was available in the deep reaches of this jungle region. He wore the typical cloth hat used in the jungles to protect against any large insect falling out of a tree on his head. Were he a river dweller, he would wear a woven palm hat.

A pair of sun glasses rested on the tip of his nose. If not to see through, they at least added to his looks. He was dressed in his very best, in what was probably his only presentable homemade shirt and trousers, barefoot of course. We had tied up our launch with plans to preach in the house of the owner of this huge plantation in the evening. I looked down at the fellow hanging onto the launch, perhaps in his one and only worldly possession, a dug-out canoe.

Again he asked, "Please come with me to see some sick people in our village."

"Where?"

"In there." He pointed with his bottom lip in the general direction of the forest, flooded out at this time of the year.

"Is it far?"

Again he pointed with his bottom lip. The lip is used to point, for either a canoe paddle, machete, or hunting shotgun usually occupied their hands. The lip did the job.

I thought about the service I was expected to hold here. "Will we be gone long?"

"No, we'll be back in a while." Translation: I could expect to be back before dark. These were the words of the man holding onto our river launch, hoping I would climb over the side into his tiny canoe.

We are having this conversation before eight o'clock in the morning. With my medicine box and another box with few instruments, I climbed down into the canoe. Triumphant to have the doctor aboard, he paddled away with my help.

Dug-outs have a little wooden keel under the stern. Steered from the bow, the one paddling has full control of the zigzag between the trees and around obstacles. Time in this culture is relevant only to the position of sun or moon and certain sets of stars. Jungle life subtly tells time as they observe certain animals or birds, the different kinds of monkeys, owls, and their typical calls during the night.

I think of these things I have observed even to the change in the crickets' sound that foretells rain or a clear night. Time stretches as our canoe moves on through the flooded forest to a place he said was "right in there."

We finally arrived "there." I climbed from the canoe, rather stiff. It's good it was "right in there." I fear to think what it would be like if he had told me his folk were quite a way in the forest. To me they were, but not to him where life seems timeless. This man was looked upon by his people as quite the hero to get this famous doctor to this little huddle of chagrined and abandoned folk.

The kiddies peeked around their mommies to see this man from the outside world. The men were stand-offish. I warmed up the villagers by thanking the man who brought me and recognizing his courageous effort to go for me. Winning confidence was my first challenge. I opened my box of instruments and medicines. Curiosity got the best of a couple of the kiddies. I played on the mystery of what was in the box. Ignoring their probing curiosity, I pulled out the

stethoscope and listened to my own heart.

"What does he hear?" One courageous kid listened to my heart. Pretty soon they were all around. Then, the consulting began.

These scenarios always hit me hard. I never got used them. It hurt to see the suffering, even being able to help. There were so many like these I could never get to and wondered if anyone else would. Treatment was non-stop. Time flew. By mid afternoon, I asked my canoe pilot to carry me back to the river and our mission launch. I was tired and drained of strength. It had been non-stop caring. On the stern of the launch, I dipped a few buckets of water from the river, and this quick "shower" revived me.

The preaching at this rubber plantation was informal and in an easy atmosphere. I climbed into my hammock on board our launch, thankful that the Lord had given me the privilege to serve Him once more.

But the eyes of the LORD are on those who fear him, on those whose hope is in his unfailing love.

Psalm 33:18 (NIV)

Chapter 12: "GOD NEVER LOOK ON HIM"

"Lime Tree Coast" sits high on the river bluff at the end of the serpentine waterway (*igarapé*) from the Lake of the Great Snail. Here it met the muddy waters of the Madeira River. For six months of the year, the water flowed into the lake. The level stayed high because the river poured into the lake during rainy season. It also brought a variety of fish and fowl.

Then everything changed for the next six months as the water flowed out of the lake. When it did, it changed the appearance of the once-flooded jungles. We lived at the upper end of Great Snail Lake in a simple house made of palm leaf thatch sitting upon wooden stilts. This waterway brought me out of the lake and connected us to the river-world outside.

I climbed to the top of Lime Tree bluff and enjoyed the beautiful view over the river. Sixty feet below, the river churned along as I watched and caught my breath. I had carried my wooden box with medical and dental instruments up to this point. I also brought some very basic medications not usually found in these remote places. My meeting was to be with Senhor Francisco, since he was to be the "go-between" for this visit. I had no idea what to expect. Life was full of surprises. He lived in one of the houses at the very top of this river bluff.

I reflected on a night here at an earlier time.

I had been this way one night when a man invited me to his table for a meal. He was an "old timer" known as Senhor Sebastian. To him, the law was his power to control otherwise unruly and violent men who worked for him in one way or another, mostly another. They would, of course, do his bidding. His rule was that any means necessary to accomplish the desired end was justifiable: rule by force. In a sense, I was in a den of thieves.

Whatever interest this Sr. Sebastian had, he wanted to hear from me. He sat at the head of the table and placed me on his right. About ten of his henchmen sat along the two sides of the long table, replete with all sorts of fish and game. The men got noisy and raucous. Suddenly, Sr. Sebastian pulled out his revolver from his belt and slammed it on the table between his plate and mine. "Shut your mouths. I'm talking with this man!" he roared. Silence reigned and the revolver lay quietly on the table. No longer was a peep heard from anyone.

But, now a different time, a different purpose. Here I was near Sr. Francisco's house. I set up a table for my instruments and medicines under some trees with plenty of shade. There were lines of people waiting for my medical services. We also put a bench in the shade–my dental chair.

These people had a reputation for frequent, wild parties in the jungle. Among those receiving my care were a couple of very scared little boys. They had probably heard some of the horror stories of teeth being dug out with scissors or by knife point. They had never had a tooth pulled with anesthesia and had no idea what it was like. A sympathetic teenager came beside the tearful little boy and comforted him while I applied the anesthesia. I later commented to Sr. Francisco how the gentle teenager showed compassion to the younger boy.

"It would seem so to you." Sr. Francisco's response showed his skepticism. "Some weeks ago there was a dance. As you know, these guys carry their shoes there and only put them on their feet when they dance. This fellow's shoes were under the bench. Another fellow just took them without asking, put them on, and danced with a gal. This teenager you thought sympathetic was so furious the other fellow had used his shoes and had not even asked permission to use them. After the dance, he waited on the trail for the one who used his shoes, and blasted him in the stomach with a shotgun. The young man who borrowed the shoes died a horrible, agonizing death." As I had so often observed, no justice reached these places.

It was a very long day of performing a lot of dental work and patient consultations. The consultations were done while I was removing teeth or waiting for anesthetic to take effect on someone's mouth.

Sr. Francisco invited me to sit at his table which overflowed with delicious game from the jungle, fish from the river and all sorts of fruits. He had really put out the "feed bag." Wow! And was I ever hungry!

Surrounded by idols in each corner of the room, I decided to ask him a leading question about God. Then I asked if any of his relatives lived nearby. I was listening for some glimmer of interest in the Gospel I represented with my life.

He turned to me. "I have a brother who lives down by the river. What a shame that God never looked on him with favor."

Yes, I reflected, *like you who think of yourself so materially well off. Many trade what they are for what they want.*

My heart gave a leap. I somehow felt that through all of this hard work providing medical and dental help to the people, this remark was God's answer.

The next time I navigated this coast of the river in the mission launch, I moved into the river port in front of the humble palm thatch house of Sr. Francisco's brother, Sr. Adonias. It was late afternoon, and I hoped to just greet the family and move on to my lake entrance and home.

To my surprise, when I greeted the family they asked me to please stay on and explain the Bible to them. We met around the light of a yellow, smoky kerosene open-wick lantern. A noisy crowd gathered outside. I imagine they had heard the big diesel launch, so the gang was bent on causing confusion.

I asked the family if they wanted me to continue, since they could suffer extreme consequences from some of these ruffians. They pleaded with me to keep teaching. That night, unrequested by me, each family member made a profession of faith in Jesus as their Savior.

In God's own time, this family migrated to the town of Humaitá, where they became some of the initial members of the fledging congregation. Sr. Adonias proved to be a true example of Christ in the community. His wife Dirce became a very good Sunday School teacher. Many others from along the river, who knew us or had heard of us, eventually moved to this town. A number of them also became followers of the Lord Jesus.

God has said it many times, that power belongs to him (and also, O Lord, steadfast love belongs to you). He rewards each one of us according to what our works deserve.

Psalm 62:11 (TLB)

Chapter 13: STRANGERS IN THE NIGHT

In the Amazon, a typical cultural diversion happens around the religious festivities of a "saint's day," of which there are plenty to go around. Some are celebrated simultaneously in various places. This incident I describe took place on the Madeira River near our home on Great Snail Lake.

Many canoes would tie up in the river port. The owners climbed to the top of the bluff and popped in on the festivities. On one of these occasions, men came downriver in a canoe with a woven palm thatch covering (*igarité*) to bury the body they were carrying in a nearby cemetery. The body was wrapped in an old hammock. Only the rich had a coffin. One man piloted from the stern while the other did most of the paddling from the bow.

The noise of the festivities wafted out over the river. These two guided their canoe in among the many, tied it up with a jungle vine, and went up the carved clay stairs to the top of the river bluff and the party. Their silent passenger remained in the covered canoe, comfortably wrapped up in the hammock. The corpse reposed on a slightly raised set of boards above any water that might be in the bottom of the canoe. One wouldn't want the body to get wet.

Being ahead of schedule, there was no way they would enter the cemetery at night to bury the body, hammock and all. The two decided they would bury their "passenger" at first light.

While many were fully animated and tanked up with the local brew, one, already on wobbly legs, made his way down the dirt steps to the port. He probably couldn't locate his canoe, but that covered canoe looked pretty good to him. He crawled in under the palm canopy and snuggled up next to the one rolled up in the hammock and went to sleep.

Roosters announced the coming dawn. The two men from that covered canoe felt it was time they were on their way. It was still dark, but it would be light by the time they reached the cemetery downriver. They paddled out into the main current of the river that would carry them more quickly to the cemetery.

They were themselves pretty well "tanked up" on the local brew. The drunk sleeping beside the corpse began to make noise and move. Not aware that the drunk had snuggled up to the corpse, the two men were convinced that the body was coming back to life. Scared half to death, they jumped into the river and swam for the shore. The two under the palm canopy were left to their own resources. The drunk and the corpse made fine bedfellows to be discovered somewhere downriver where the canoe drifted to the shore.

NO HELP FROM ANY SAINT

On another night way downriver, the "saint festivities" ended differently. Below Alligator Island was a point of land called Singing Rooster. This long, narrow peninsula divided the strong currents of the Madeira River. At the lower end of Alligator Island the river current converges in front of Singing Rooster and often created a whirlpool feared and avoided by riverboats.

The party in honor of a "saint" was going full blast through the night. The elderly ladies took care of the children away from the noise and debauchery, far back in the jungle, where all the kiddies slept in their hammocks under mosquito nets. Every once in a while, one of the ladies would trek the short trail to the river bluff at Singing Rooster to see what was going on.

On one of these visits, the elderly lady saw a crack in the earth near to Singing Rooster. She ran to the party and warned the gang that something was going to happen as the earth was cracking open on the jungle side of the point of land of Singing Rooster. The dear lady was laughed away, and so returned to the kiddies back in the jungle house.

How much later in the night it happened is anyone's guess. Without warning, the entire point of land of Singing Rooster slid into the murky depths of the Madeira River. The whirlpool had probably eroded this land underwater. All were lost. No saint protected the revelers. The kiddies were left to be raised by the grandmas. One night's debauchery took many lives and left many orphans.

How many die unready to face eternity?

And just as it is destined that men die only once, and after that comes judgment, so also Christ died only once as an offering for the sins of many people; and he will come again, but not to deal again with our sins.

Hebrews 9:27-28 (TLB)

What makes us think that we can escape if we are indifferent to this great salvation announced by the Lord Jesus himself and passed on to us by those who heard him speak?

Hebrews 2:3 (TLB)

Chapter 14: HOME SWEET HOME ON URUAPIÁRA

From our home at the head of the Lake of the Great Snail, we could see afar. The name "Long View" fit well.

To prepare a meal was no easy trick. Barbara became pretty adept at putting together some delicious meals. The neighbour ladies were proud to know she could start from nothing and really put on a feed. Fish or fowl, there was always plenty to eat and share or salt away for a rainy day.

Home on Uruapiára, our front yard. (Guest house on right)

Barbara & friends at clinic door

Clinic and "Dr. Luis" (Alan's middle name)

David & friend in front of the kitchen with a fish. (Tambaquí)

Paca (rodent) and small tender alligator
We ate whatever the jungle or river provided, one way or another

250 lb. Tapir (from night hunt in swamp)

Cormorant–luscious when skinned and roasted.

Uruapiára life demanded being resourceful.

Diving or casting net, fish were there.

URUAPIÁRA'S "DOCTOR" AND LITTLE WOLF

Darkness drops like a curtain on the jungle. Three young fellows had hung their hammocks high in the trees, hopefully out of the jaguar's reach. In the cook pot hanging over the smoldering fire was part of an animal they hunted that day. From their hammocks they looked at the fire below. The smoke would reduce the clouds of mosquitoes. Fewer would find them up in the trees. Before dawn they would climb down from the hammocks for a cup of coffee to chase away the pre-dawn chill. And off they went, each to his trail, to carve the diagonal cuts in the bark of the rubber trees and place a little tin cup to collect the rubber milk. A second trip would be made to collect the rubber latex milk from the tiny tin cans. But that was their every day routine.

Little Wolf lay in his hammock. *How did I get where I am?* He thought back how he ran away from home and had spent thirty days crossing the jungle. In the other hammock one of his friends was shivering with a bad case of malaria (again).*And look where I am now,* he thought, not at peace with his decision.

He once lived with his mom and dad on Great Snail Lake. Why had he run away? He thought about it. A family had come to live in a palm thatch house just like everybody there on the lake. From his house on "Windy Point," Little Wolf could see their place and the canoes and riverboats that came and went. Why so many people? What was different about this family? In one way they were just like Little Wolf's people. They had no refrigerator, no gas stove. Like everyone else, they used kerosene lamps and made their fire on a clay platform above the dirt floor kitchen. This family brought nothing with them from the outside world. No modern conveniences. They got their drinking water from the brook that came out of the jungle and they washed their clothes down at the lake just like any other family.

Yet there was something different about these people. They called him "Doctor Luis." Day after day he extracted teeth and examined the sick. Sometimes he would do surgery in his little palm shack clinic to take out a small tumor, repair a gunshot or knife wound. He treated snake bites and serious illnesses common to the jungle.

Some who went to see him were his enemies, but they all went away cured. Sometimes a canoe full of people would arrive from many days' journey in hopes of being cured. Those who traveled great distances would hang their hammocks and stay in a palm house next to his. Everyone used the same outhouse on the edge of the forest behind the dirt floor kitchen. Often the people had eaten dried fish or dried meat on their travel. At night "Doctor Luis" would get into his canoe to spear fish or hunt so the sick visitors would have food.

Everyone could hear his conversations. That was the way in that culture. Palm walls didn't hold any secrets. Those who listened told

Little Wolf he talked about how he followed a living Christ. The way he cared for people and how he talked about his Jesus sounded so different. After all, we had a Christ, but ours was a dead one.

Little Wolf continued to reminisce there in his hammock. Crickets chirped a serenade. An occasional bat would swoop by. The owls hooted. He thought back.

The clash came for me when my father learned that I wanted to go to this doctor's house to listen when he talked to his patients. My father told me he would whip me, because that doctor and his family were not of our religion. I asked myself and what good is our religion if it docsn't change our life and we never know if we will really have eternal life?

That was when I decided to run away. I was almost twelve years old and would be expected to start doing a man's work in the jungle. But what if I never learned about this living Jesus?

So Little Wolf had run away to avoid the punishment he would receive if he visited the home of this family.

As Little Wolf lay in his hammock reflecting, the jungle night closed around these three with all its sounds. The fire was burning low. Little Wolf tuned his new portable radio he had purchased with the money he made working. What a special thing it was for him to own this little portable and listen to many short wave frequencies. Now he could hear programs in his Portuguese tongue. He tuned into one very different program. The voice told Little Wolf about this living Jesus.

During the night one of his two friends died of malaria. The next morning they rolled the body in the hammock and buried him there. Little Wolf knew where he would go without Jesus. Soon after that night he asked the living Jesus to be his Savior.

Although I knew of the boy living on our lake, I did not hear his story until some years later. I was speaking at the chapel service in a Bible College in the city of Manaus. A young man smiled at me the whole time. He came to me after and asked, "Dr Luis, do you remember me?"Actually we had never met, but he knew who I was.

Little Wolf then told me his story. Today he is a preacher evangelist in the Amazon region. He tells many of our Lord and his message of love, compassion and forgiveness. Who could imagine that a youngster from a remote lake in the jungles of the Amazon would grow up to become a choice servant of our God?

Jesus said,

"Let your light so shine before men that they can see your good works and glorify your Father in heaven."

Matthew 5:16 (KJV)

A MOTHER'S UNKEPT SECRET

Our palm thatch house on Great Snail Lake was like houses all around the lake and throughout the jungle. We cooked on a wood fire, had an outhouse, got our water from the stream coming out of the jungle, and washed our clothes down at the lake. I hunted and fished to put food on our table. Our lifestyle was just like the rest of the lake dwellers.

Our house could be seen from any point around this huge lake. They also knew that a man lived there who took care of their illnesses, pulled their teeth and sewed them up on occasion.

One day a lady came with her little baby. One glance told me that at least part of the problem was that both the mother and her baby were extremely dehydrated. There was no elasticity to the skin and their eyes were sunken. I could simply tell the mother that she and her baby were dehydrated, but she would go away not accepting nor understanding those terms.

So, how do I handle this situation? The key to communicating with her was to know the culture and use that knowledge to help her understand.

"Tell me about your childhood illnesses. What remedies were used to treat you?"

She told me quite a long story about a grandma and auntie treating her for fevers with tea from the cashew tree bark or holy grass, a fragrant weed also used to make tea. I proceeded to discuss the treatment with her.

"This is what I want you to do. When you get out of the hammock in the morning, don't put your feet on the cold floor (72 degrees). Put your feet right into your sandals. Don't lift the mosquito net quickly, but very slowly so you don't catch a "branch of air" (a draft of cooler air) in your lungs. Go to the kitchen (dirt floor). Be careful not to go near the clay water pot until you have a fire going. Then heat a tin of water."

By custom, the first thing she did in the morning would be to start a fire. She would fan the embers still there from the night before on the clay covered wood platform. She heated the water for coffee using a liter tin, which previously had held cooking oil. Once the fire was going, she would heat that tin of water and pour it through a cloth full of coffee grounds. The coffee would be ready for her husband when he returned from his rubber tree route some time after dawn.

"Drink a cup of very warm water the size of a condensed milk tin."

"Don't go out in the morning dew until the sun is about here," which would be about 8 a.m.

She probably wouldn't go out any earlier. I continued to come up with creative inventions for her to drink liquids such as holy weed tea and cashew bark tea throughout the day.

"Come back in a few days to tell me if you have milk enough to nurse your baby."

I wanted to find out if she believed in my "prescription." Everything that I asked her to do was routine to her culture and were ingrained habits which she already followed. Since I was aware of the customs and incorporated them in my dialogue, she understood and accepted what I told her. She did return several days later.

"Doctor, I don't know what to do!"

Uh-oh, I thought to myself.

"I'm nursing my neighbor's baby and even a friend crosses the lake in her canoe so I can nurse her baby. Still I have too much milk!"

I reviewed all the teas and other foods in her diet. I then told her to take no more tea after 3 p.m. Usually they ate fish and manioc meal by sundown, and then the family went under their nets early in the evening before the mosquitoes start to swarm.

"Lady, your milk will be a little less. But please don't tell anyone of our secret!"

She agreed, but I very well knew she would tell her story to everyone. All the women on the lake, even the midwives with all their fables, would want to know what the doctor at the end of the lake had prescribed. The word got out. I never treated another case on this lake of a mother or baby with dehydration.

Know the culture of the people with whom you communicate.

Knowledge applied is wisdom. Package it in an irresistible art form which each will want to open.

"For I know the plans I have for you," declares the LORD, "plans to prosper you and not to harm you, plans to give you hope and a future."

Jeremiah 29:11 (NIV)

Chapter 15: AN ADVERSARY
ON GREAT SNAIL LAKE

Our home was simple and serene, a palm thatch house on the shore of the biggest lake of any number of smaller ones in this bend of the Madeira River. The lake connected to the river by a winding waterway. Six months of the year, the rising Madeira River held back the flow of the lake into the river. As the river rose, so did the level of the lake. Waterways back in the jungle helped sustain this high water which flooded vast areas of jungle around the lake. The next six months, the lake slowly lowered as the river level dropped and the water flowed out to the lowering river. Waterways and one river fed into the lake year round. Fish, reptiles, birds and all sorts of wildlife showed a six-month cycle of change from highest to lowest level.

Our house of palm thatch sat on stilts so, although far enough from the edge of the lake at low water, the peak of rainy season could raise the lake level to come right up to our house at high water. Fortunately alligators didn't climb stairs.

Our life style was the same as everyone else's who lived around the lake. We washed our clothes at the lake shore. We carried our water for drinking and cooking from a crystal clear stream that flowed out of the jungle. Palm walls and a thatch palm roof gave us a front room and another for our hammocks. The floor was made of split palm logs nailed to cross pieces. Under our hammocks with their mosquito nets, we had covered the palm log floor with a woven palm mat so the mosquitoes couldn't get through. We connected these two rooms by planks to the kitchen of hard packed dirt. Barbara cooked on an open and often smoky fire on a raised wooden platform covered with clay.

Behind the kitchen on the edge of the forest was our outhouse. No plumbing was needed. We had no kerosene refrigerator and neither did anyone else living by us or in the region. Any game or fish we did not cook was salted immediately and kept for another meal or shared with our neighbor, a little way along a path.

Near our palm house and slightly closer to our trail to the lake port, I had a small palm-leaf shed three feet off the ground on stilts which was my "clinic." People came by riverboat and canoe. Some paddled for a day or two seeking medical help. On any given day, I extracted dozens of teeth. While the anesthesia was taking effect or I was "working out" a tooth, I would be asking others about their illnesses. In this ambience everybody listened in and watched. Explanations on nutrition and hygiene were inserted in the conversations. Occasionally the person I cared for would require a bit of surgery, which I did on the spot.

The clinic on Uruapiára

One rainy day I lifted the woven palm-thatch "window" which we could prop open with a stick when the rain came without too much wind. I saw a canoe coming across the lake with two men. The one in the back was a big muscular fellow. In the bow was a scrawny little man. I watched them as they climbed out of their canoe at our lakeside port and came up the trail to the house. They were both armed. The big fellow had a shotgun which he kept ready to use. The little man had a revolver and a knife tucked into his belt. When they clapped to announce their arrival, I could see a potentially life-threatening situation unfold. I asked God for wisdom and opened the door, the only item made of wood in the house.

There at the bottom of the ladder with only three steps up to the house, stood these men still bearing their firearms and knife. I invited them up into the house. They did not disarm themselves. Bad news! When they came in and sat down on the board bench along the palm wall, I commented that they must be cold from being out on the lake in the rain.

I called to Barbara to prepare some hot chocolate on the wood fire and some crackers. Barbara took a "loaf" of chocolate we had baked from the fruit of the cocoa bean, and with a fish tongue she grated the chocolate into powder and mixed it with hot water and sugar.

Barbara had prepared this block of pure chocolate earlier. The process consisted of wrapping raw chocolate-bean pulp that had been pummeled in a hollowed-out wooden stump. Then wrapped in a banana leaf, Barbara baked it over the fire in an upturned five gallon can that was her "oven." She served these two men the hot chocolate and crackers. All this time I was praying for wisdom.

The moment of reckoning had come. They had finished the customary gesture of hospitality, being served something. "In what way can I serve you?" I asked.

The little man replied arrogantly, "I am the dentist on the lake." This was an obvious challenge since he knew I had been extracting piles of teeth daily.

God gave me a response I never dreamed of. "What good news this is to me to know that you are a dentist," I exclaimed. (His blood-stained shirt attested to it.) "I am only a Pastor and have been pulling a tooth or two." I offered to *loan* him needles and anesthesia. He informed me that he didn't use anesthesia. He pulled the teeth out with the point of a scissor or a pair of pliers. That was a good way to break teeth and leave painful roots, if not a massive infection. After some more chit chat they left peacefully.

Some days later a group of about eight arrived in a large canoe. They had come from a great distance out on the Madeira. Next to our house we had a "guest house" which was nothing but a one-room palm leaf shelter with a dirt floor that could accommodate many hammocks with their ever present mosquito nets. The visitors would use our outhouse and cook on our wood fire clay platform. They arrived under a light rain that continued into the night. The only food these dear folk had eaten all day was the dried fish and manioc meal they had brought with them on their canoe trip to the lake. They were certainly hungry, so I went to get them some food in the jungle.

With rain on the water, I could not see to spear fish. I had no more powder to reload my shotgun shells, so I grabbed my 38 caliber long barrel revolver and paddled off in my dugout. In some backwater I found a roost of wild pigeons up in the trees. Holding the flashlight behind my head so I could aim the revolver, I shot at one pigeon. Immediately I turned off the flashlight so the pigeons would settle down again. Using eight bullets I shot eight of these wild pigeons.

Paddling back, I plucked them all. When I had the pigeons split open and gutted, they were ready to roast over the coals of the wood fire. My neighbor came over from his place nearby in the jungle. He observed from the sound that I had not used a shotgun to kill the pigeons. "No," I replied, "I only had bullets for my 38 revolver."

He looked at the pigeons and said, "But you hit them all in the head!" So I explained that if the 38 bullet hit the pigeon in the body, there wouldn't be much meat left on the bird. I had been taught how to gently squeeze the trigger by my older brother when I was a kid. These folk ate the roasted pigeons with manioc meal, which we ourselves use and always had plenty on hand. The next day I began to treat this canoe-full of people that had come so far.

A week later I was called to another place on the lake to help a lady give birth to her first baby. While I was with the woman behind the palm partition that separates the one room from the front area, someone came up the wooden ladder on the other side to the front room. I could hear him working the action of a revolver. Click. Snap. Click. Snap.

Another set of footsteps came up the ladder. The first voice said to the second, "Does that doctor in there know how to repair guns? Mine isn't working well. I tried shooting someone and the gun didn't fire."

The second voice replied, "Hey, don't mess with that guy. I heard he shoots pigeons in the dark with a revolver and always hits them in the head." (The use of a flashlight had been omitted from the retelling of the story.)

Well, they say that stories grow with the telling. No one ever challenged us again while we lived on the lake. God uses ways we may think strange to protect us from evil men.

Because they trust in him, he helps them and delivers them from the plots of evil men.

Psalm 37:40 (TLB)

Chapter 16: FIRE ON BOARD

Numerous sources of water flow into the Lake of the Great Snail. One of these waterways was called "Red Earth." Red it wasn't. This one poured volumes of crystalline waters into the lake. Ironically the name came from the very red clay at the port close to where this spring gushed out of the earth to form the waterway.

I was on a quick errand across our lake and into this crystal clear waterway that bubbled out of the ground far back in the jungle. My daughter Beth and her little friend Maria went along for the ride. We were in the sheet metal boat I had made which was small, light, and it "flew like the wind." It was powered by a 35 HP outboard motor. The little boat served us well and skimmed over the water. Frequently the front cowling on the outboard needed to be removed to adjust the carburetors and to retard the magneto a bit because of the poor gasoline, which was mixed with oil as in any two-cycle engine.

Travel was a bit precarious along the Red Earth waterway because the current was very strong. We could see the turtles that had secured themselves on the bottom, wedged under logs to prevent the current from carrying them away. The water was cold and crystalline. The current became stronger as we navigated closer to the place where the water churned up from the jungle floor. We tied up at a little dock, and I turned off the outboard motor. Soon the time came to return to our home on the lake. I left the boat tied to the dock in a loose loop while I tried to start the motor, or else the current would carry the boat into the jungle overhang. If we were tossed into that overhang by the current, we would find ourselves in a lot of trouble.

When I tried to start the outboard motor, yellow flames burst from the throats of the two carburetors. What should I do? Toss Beth and Maria overboard into the current? The two little girls knew how to swim, but it was dangerous in that strong current. There were logs and roots. Dense jungle draped its curtain to the water's edge. Life preservers were nonexistent. Should I dive overboard myself? The options seemed to flash through my mind like lightening. Although it seemed like ages, these thoughts zipped by within fractions of a second. I lived conditioned to *what if.*

In one motion I tore my perspired shirt (the material was old and weak) off my back and stuffed it in the throats of the carburetors. No mechanical damage occurred. I pulled on the starter cord once more and the motor sprang in to life. I slipped the rope loop from the dock put the outboard in gear and away we went, scooting over the turtles sleeping under the logs in the bottom. The wildlife we left behind probably watched us from the jungle, glad to have us gone.

"...but whoever listens to me will live in safety and be at ease, without fear of harm."

Proverbs 1:33 (NIV)

Chapter 17: A MAN CALLED JULIAN

They later found timbers in the jungle that he had hewn square with a long axe to then saw into boards. That night I carried his body wrapped in a simple hammock down to the river edge. My boat would take him home to his family upriver. It was a night to remember.

Days later I could put the pieces together. On what was to be his last day, Pastor Julian, well known to all, had gone around the village saying goodbye and making sure he was leaving no forgotten purchase unpaid. People asked, "Pastor Julian, are you going to travel?" His reply was always the same. "I am going away for good."

I was home. The kids were safe in their hammocks under the mosquito nets. I was headed there soon myself. Barbara had finished up in our humble little kitchen which required careful steps over the rickety, uneven floor. Of a sudden a voice called outside our door. "Pastor, come quick. Something has happened to Pastor Julian." I ran behind his neighbor the few minutes down the dirt track to Pastor Julian's palm house.

I found him inert, lying on the rough split palm-log floor. His dear wife sat there observing in such a tranquil repose. Pastor Julian had slipped away to answer God's call.

Julian had returned to their palm leaf thatch home after his circuit of the village. He and his wife had their simple supper of rice, fish, and manioc meal. Then they moved to their front room, the only other rooms being the kitchen and the one in which they hung their hammocks under the mosquito nets. The neighbor who sent for me had been there with them, each tasting their sweet *cafezinho*.

Upon finishing his little demitasse cup, Julian said, "Life has been full of blessings, and now it's time to go." He just rolled off the wooden bench where he had been and so softly spread out on the floor.

Who was this man that the Lord called to heaven in such a peaceful manner? I met him shortly after arriving in the village where strong opposition to our Evangelical presence was blatantly manifest. Who we were and why we were there was a task to communicate graciously and with tender care. After all, we were Ambassadors of the Living God. Julian with his seventy-eight years, born here in the Amazon, had wise counsel to offer.

When we moved to Humaitá, we walked into what could have been a real hornet's nest. Pastor Julian saved us much grief. People were accustomed to a multi party political system. Candidates that came up our river seeking election to whatever office would try for votes. They promised potential voters a machete, some yards of cloth or whatever. Unabashed, the person would promise their vote. When the next candidate for another party came along, the scenario would repeat itself. More promises and more handouts.

By a similar mindset, people were locked into a system of social conformity in a society where all social exchange and interaction was based on subservience to the authority of the religious system. That aberration was missed by most. Jesus said, "I am the way, the truth and the life. No man can come to God the Father but by me." (St John 14.6) The tenet of any system is either the authority of any man or the absolute authority of God and His inerrant Word.

This village of 800 was subservient to a bishop, three priests, and twelve nuns of an Italian order of their patron, Dom Bosco. The presence of another voice or a different point view of life was considered a threat to the system in control. In reality there was the municipal government's mayor, who walked softly on the premise that "one hand washes the other." Consequently, municipal and religious authority maintained a symbiotic or communalistic relationship of smiles and apparent cordiality. However, strong tensions flowed underneath this façade.

We took up residence in Humaitá in a ramshackle house near what served as telegraph and post office. Soon after arriving, we learned that an elderly couple had moved into a nice palm thatch house about ten minutes' walk from our place. People called him Pastor. I met him and took the attitude that I would do nothing in the local culture without first inquiring of him. Julian, self taught, never spent a day in school but was well read and had a very good command of Portuguese grammar.

Julian informed me of an event that turned out to be a "bad trip" as regards a true representation of the Biblical basis of eternal salvation. A couple of "preachers" had come uninvited from Manaus to "show these people something." It is no wonder the Bishop Dom Michael would be upset if he thought we were "cut from the same cloth," that is, of the same approach as these "preachers."

Each night they proclaimed one point of their "message." If you follow us (the Jesus we preach) then:

1st night - You won't need to ask the Bishop for a food supplement.

2nd night - Your kids won't have to study in the parochial school.

3rd night - You won't have to go the nun's hospital when you're sick.

By the end of the five days, they were "selling fish" in the name of religion.

The implication to a multi-party political system mentality was that they would hand out food, start a school, build a hospital and bring in doctors and on and on.

Since when is any of this nonsense to be spoken as if it were inferred to be Jesus' teaching? He was crystal clear. Time and again Jesus said that in essence "he who has ears to hear let him hear."

Julian, as a young man, met a travelling book seller who passed through his region of the river where he then lived. The man had many volumes, but of only one book. The price was very accessible. Books were a rare thing as then so few had learned to read the pages. Julian was told that this book was a collection of sixty-six writings all under the guidance of one. They covered a period of about 1500 years. The book began with the creation of the world, related many adventures of ancient kings, a book of poetry, one of wise sayings, all the way to the life of Jesus. It concluded with how the world as we know it would end.

Julian had bought a Bible. He took it home, showed it to his father and asked his father if it was okay to keep. His father replied, "If this is God's book, we will soon know. You know how to read, so starting from the beginning. Every night you will read to us." And so the reading continued night after night at the light of an open-wick, yellow, smoky *lamparina*.

They had read through the Old Testament group of thirty-nine books. Upon arriving early from the jungle one day, Julian sought out his father. His mother informed him, "A man of that book came by and invited those who believe in Jesus as their Savior to publicly declare this by baptism."

Julian asked his mother if he could go where his father was at a nearby rubber plantation upriver. With his mother's consent this twenty-four year old went down to the river, got in his canoe, and paddled away to the plantation. Tying up the canoe and sticking the paddle in brush out of the sun, Julian went up the river bank to the plantation to find his father.

He greeted the owner of the rubber plantation and inquired of this man, usually referred to as "The Colonel" because of his authority over everyone. He explained to Julian that the man of the book had taken a group of people back to a lake to "dunk them" and feed them to the piranha.

The "Colonel" proceeded to mock those who intended to follow Jesus. He said some very vile things and began to blaspheme God. Julian was shocked, and with a good basis in God's book.

He said to the Colonel, "Sir, I have read much about the God of this book. He hears and sees all. He hears your vile comments against Him. He does not let these things go unpunished. Please stop what you are saying, for God is a righteous God."

With that comment, Julian set off to find the group back by the lake. The "Colonel" continued his tirade and scoffed all the more. His group of workers observed as he put on quite a show.

Nightfall was closing in as the group returned from the lake to the river port of the plantation. Everywhere men were shouting, looking for the Colonel, who seemed to have disappeared.

There came a shout. "I've found him!

And there he was. The Colonel sat against a tree, "stiff as a brick" dead as a stone! The comments of the workers recalled his "spitting in the face of God" and seemed to feel "he got what was coming to him."

Young Julian had lived in remote and lawless reaches of the Amazon jungle. Shortly after his conversion to follow Christ, Julian was trekking a jungle trail to a nearby group of houses where he wanted to tell the people how he came to be a follower of Jesus. Early on, he was seen to be an itinerant evangelist even before the phrase was in use. He was going over a trail to a group of houses where he had invited folk to meet to hear about the God of the Book.

On the trail a man lay in wait to ambush him because Julian had "left his religion." As he jumped out on the trail the man said, "I am going to kill you!"

Julian replied, "Very well, but you should give a condemned man his last dying wish."

Mr. Shotgun asked, "And what is your dying wish?"

Julian invited him along to hear him preach about Jesus.

"When I have finished preaching, then you can shoot me." Mr. Shotgun agreed, and off they went together. At the end of Julian's talk with the people, he asked if anyone wanted to follow Jesus as he had done. The first one to declare his faith in the Lord was the intended assassin. Mr. Shotgun came to the front of the group, tears streaming down his face. He asked Julian to forgive him for the intent to kill him. Mr. Shotgun became a true follower of Jesus.

On a later occasion, Julian was speaking at a palm house on stilts (six or seven feet off the ground) back in the jungle. Most houses were built this way. Chickens, pigs, ducks and all lived, squawked and grunted under the house. A set of round logs was the ladder up to the floor of the house. It was the house of one who was now a follower of Jesus. The man was known to have been given to violence before he turned the rule of his life into the hands of the Lord. Quite a noisy crowd had gathered outside his house.

Finally he stepped to the open doorway and looked down at the crowd of noisemakers and critics. The man pulled his big machete from where it was slid into the palm thatch and waived it menacingly at the crowd and said, "Look, I have been converted to be a follower of the Lord Jesus, but my machete is not converted, so if you want to meet my machete just come on and give it a try."

The crowd calmed down. Julian spoke and many heard of the pardon for sin and new life in Christ of which the owner of this simple palm thatch house was a certain example.

Many are the unwritten chapters in the life of Pastor Julian. As I ran the river that night with his body wrapped in a hammock, I knew he was in heaven with the Lord he had served so faithfully. I was merely taking the shell of what had been to his family upriver. It was at dark when I arrived as the bearer of news one does not wish to carry.

Early dawn found us at work preparing a coffin. No one's body here remains out of ground more than the extreme limit of twenty-four hours. Less time better. With an axe, an adz, hammer, and saw we set out to make what would hold the remains of this man. But his legacy would not be buried with his bones. The little cemetery plot was surrounded by barbed wire to keep jungle animals from digging there. From where we stood to say our last goodbyes, we looked out over the mighty Madeira River. That morning it seemed so serene, flowing smoothly on its way.

I asked myself, *When I go, what will I leave behind? A life that served others, a heritage, kids and grandkids who will follow Jesus?* Have you ever asked yourself how you will step into eternity?

It's a question. And one day God will ask you.

There are books that inform.

There are books that reform

There are books that deform

There is one book that transforms – God's Book, the Bible.

Trust what God says.

For the word of the LORD is right and true;
he is faithful in all he does.

Psalm 33: (NIV)

Chapter 18: AN AMBASSADOR, BUT FOR WHOM?

An ambassador is a diplomatic agent of the highest rank sent by a sovereign to reside in a foreign land to represent the one who sent him and to build relationships in the name of that one by whom he has been sent.

Our family had just moved two days upriver to this village, new to us, from the lake of the Great Snail where we had lived. The village was very hostile to us, as we did not identify with the prevalent religion. Merchants were ordered not to sell to us, but merchants like to sell. People avoided greeting us on the few streets.

A store owner, Dona Antonieta, was deeply involved in the community and the leader of a sewing club. The group made items for the poorer families, especially items which a woman would need at the time of giving birth.

I had met Dona Antonieta two years before, when my colleagues and I visited this village to seek God's guidance regarding the possibility of evangelizing people one on one. I hoped to see a few of the followers of Jesus eventually form as a group. On that visit, we three men had arrived on the mission's diesel launch. We tied up in the river port with access to the steps to the top of the river bluff. We expected to be observed by the town's people.

During that visit I met Dona Antonieta in her store and learned that she served meals at a table in her little shop. I contracted meals for the days we would be in town. The menu could include any one of many kinds of fish, tapir or jaguar meat, jungle fowl, or a large rodent called *paca*. She prepared noon and evening meals for us each day. In the morning we had coffee and bread from the local store on the boat.

I went to the covered market where villagers would go to see what was available, all of it to cook from scratch. There were roots that people had planted and all kinds of river fish, big and small, piled up on one counter. You could purchase a whole small fish or just a few pounds of a bigger fish. The meat counter might have wild water buffalo available. These buffalo have gone wild since the time when the Spanish explorers brought them from Asia centuries ago. At the meat counter some options might include tapir, red panther, a big ground bird the size of a wild turkey, called *mutun* (moo-toon), delicious and all white meat. I passed the time just looking around, trying to appear as inconspicuous as possible and so attract no attention. I overheard a conversation behind me. "Yes, the Bishop is going to excommunicate Dona Antonieta if she serves anymore meals to those evangelical men that are here on that river launch."

I delivered this news to my colleagues, and we agreed that there was no way we wanted to bring any discomfort or coercion on Dona

Antonieta. I informed her that we had a sudden change of plans and were traveling downriver to a big rubber plantation.

We would no longer be able to enjoy any more of her delicious meals, but perhaps she could cook for us sometime in the future. I saw such a look of relief and peace come over this woman. We had pulled her "out of the fire" from the Bishop's threat of excommunication.

A few years after that visit, we arrived as a family to this village. We moved in to an old, dilapidated house we rented next to the "post office" We began buying Dona Antonieta's bread, baked in her round wood-fired clay oven. We bought rice, beans, sugar, salt, and other necessities in her shop. Dona Antonieta had a chance to observe our kids, very Brazilian and very polite.

Barbara easily made friends with Dona Antonieta and was soon an ambassadress with the women of the sewing club Dona Antonieta directed. It seemed that the community was accepting us as one of them. Soon Mother's Day would come. The sewing club held a special program each year when they would give out all of the items they made such as small rag rugs, diapers, cloths to the poorer women of the village. The event would take place in the "Bishop's Auditorium," which was set up like a theater with a stage and curtains. Who was chosen to speak to the village women about motherhood? Barbara!

I was in the wings behind the closed curtain where Barbara stood waiting for the curtain to open. And who should appear there behind the curtain with us while I was taking Barbara's picture? You guessed it. Dom Michael, the bishop. After all, it was his theater.

When he saw Barbara, he turned to look at me. I smiled. He was at a loss how to handle the matter. He was not happy. On various occasions I'd had conversations with Bishop Dom Michael. I understood that he was sincerely fulfilling what he understood to be his role in life. He could not concur with Jesus' declaration in the book of St. John when He said, "I am the way, the truth and the life. No man can come to my Father in heaven except through me." When we discussed these matters, the bishop insisted on many "add-ons."

Standing there in the theater, he could see that we had been accepted by the community. As the Lord's ambassadors, we had to be careful not to do anything that might offend someone. Barbara's presentation was spectacular and won the hearts of the women with rounds of applause at the end of her speech. I was floating in the clouds over the day's outcome.

Our calling was to be imitators of Christ, a character trait that just keeps on giving. We needed to act (not react) in a way that people could see Him in us. Yes, even those who knew we did not align with their point of view. Still they watched.

We are Christ's ambassadors. God is using us to speak to you: we beg you, as though Christ himself were here pleading with you, receive the love he offers you, be reconciled to God.

2 Corinthians 5:20 (TLB)

Chapter 19: MISTER MAGOO
AND THE DOCTOR MEET

Hands clapped in front of the house we rented in the village. Clapping hands came before electricity and doorbells. I opened the rickety door onto the flat surface called a sidewalk. I invited the hand clapper into what we called the living room of this ramshackle house.

When he stepped through the door, my first thought was, *Here is a tall, thin version of the old cartoon character, Mr. Magoo.* Very frail and wearing a felt hat, his very thick eyeglass lenses were not to be missed.

I invited him to sit in one of our woven vine chairs, cool and comfortable. After some chit chat, we went to the matter of his visit. News travels fast along the river. He had heard that a doctor from some days downriver had come to live in this village of 800 people.

The word was out that this man was not of the traditional religion, thus was relegated to the "off limits" list of prohibitions for the "faithful." Nonetheless the word travelled quickly by the "jungle vine" (word of mouth). He had heard that it was the doctor and his family that did so much for the diseases and teeth of those downriver in the lake of the Great Snail, where they last lived.

I did the usual exam of heart, lungs, blood pressure, and many questions that almost always began to reveal a pattern. Mr. "Magoo" touched me in some way. Jesus had compassion on people. As His representative, that concern for people lodged in me. Little would be the motivation if one only "took pity" on the suffering.

Step one for most of those I treated over the years was to gain their confidence. A trust relationship was often the key to learning what symptoms they would tell and the signs an examination might reveal. In talking around, I learned that "Mr. Magoo," who lived across the river, had a flashlight battery-powered short-wave radio.

I wrote out two prescriptions in block letters. One I told him was to improve his physical well being. I smiled at him as I passed him the second prescription. "This is for your soul."

He looked at me with a quizzical expression. I prescribed an early morning short-wave radio program in Portuguese to which he should listen. He would then know the way to God. To follow would still be a choice for him to make.

The clock of life ticked on. We left this village where initially we experienced much opposition. We became part of the local culture and made every effort to present a clear and simple explanation of who Jesus Christ is according to what God says in His Holy Book. We departed the village of 800 or so, leaving behind a small congregation of those who decided to follow Christ.

Years later, the congregation had grown. They sold their first location on the river front and moved to the center of the town as it spread back through the jungle where I used to hunt. They had acquired a large tract of land. Population has at this writing reached around 30,000. The church pays their pastor, has educational facilities through high school, and supports three missionary couples in tribes in the region.

I was the keynote speaker for the church's missionary conference one year.

I chose to sit among the congregation, often to better sense those to whom I would speak. As God so worked it, He placed me on one of the benches next to a woman who turned and smiled. The service was yet to begin so I asked her, "Do I know you?" In the culture I could not ask, "Who are you?"

To my surprise, she said: "You don't know me but, you knew my father." (My Mr. Magoo.) She went on to tell me that her father had come back home across the river in his canoe from his consultation with me. The following morning, all were awakened to listen to a radio program on short wave from 4 am until 6 am.

"As Father aged, became weaker, and his health was failing fast, he called all us children together. He said, 'I am going to a place Jesus, who is my Savior, promised to prepare for me. I want you children to move across the river to the village and go to hear this Pastor who first told me about Jesus.' Many a leaf of a calendar year had fallen from then till now." The lady told me that she and her brothers had all married, were followers of Jesus, and brought their kids to Sunday school.

The church had filled and the service began. God gave me great joy to speak for Him. That day I looked at a church that supported its pastor and three missionaries in jungle tribes. The church administered a day school. The "little village" was the county seat nearing thirty thousand population with five evangelical churches.

As Jim Elliot, who gave his life to reach the Auca Indian tribe far west of where we lived, had said, "He is no fool to give up what he cannot keep, to gain what he cannot lose."

And what of the stories of others touched by God along the rivers and lakes of that little part of the Amazon where we lived? Who knows? God does! He keeps the books.

The one who calls you is faithful, and he will do it.

1 Thessalonians 5:24 (NIV)

Chapter 20: A PAGE FROM AN AMBASSADOR

One of the nuns sent for me to come quickly to the "Nun's Hospital," as it was known, to attend to an emergency situation. It was the very first time they had ever sent for me. The reputation we had and the need of the nuns had developed into a set of circumstances like none other.

I had no idea of the danger I was in when I stepped into the court yard of the "Nun's Hospital." A woman whom I had treated during her pregnancy had ample warning from me that she should abide by a strict diet as she could have severe difficulties during her labor and birth of her child. She was a good candidate for eclampsia, but I didn't go into explanations as to the severity of it. When for the first time I was summoned to the hospital and told to bring my delivery kit, I heard threatening remarks as I entered the outer courtyard. "A believer may get in our hospital, but he won't make it out again!" *Crente*, believer, is what a Protestant was called.

When I arrived to the delivery area, I found the mother-to-be whom I so feared to be prone to eclampsia. There was mass confusion. The nuns had tried every trick they thought they knew. They had been at it since the previous day. Now with a very complicated situation, they called me in to do the delivery.

Just as I got to her, she exhaled a ghastly gurgle and stopped breathing. Froth poured from her mouth. I placed gauze rolls between her teeth, removed the froth, and began mouth to mouth respiration.

Then I gave her a good stout sock on her sternum and with a gasp—miracle of miracles—she began to breath.

I went for the baby with DeLee low forceps. I wanted the little rascal out before her blood pressure began to soar. To my own sadness, the baby had died in the womb. From what I could observe, this happened yesterday or before. No one would really tell me how long she had been in the delivery area.

Like the spider medicine of a previous story, incrimination is not my role. I did get out of the hospital unscathed. It would seem that enough was heard of my actions to alleviate their sentiments about followers of Jesus.

Representing our God, who had sent us here, produced some interesting situations more clearly seen in hind sight. Sister Klara, a very elderly nun, sent a boy to call me to the hospital. This hospital identified with the order whose Patron was Dom Bosco, an educator of the Italian Silesian Order.

Sister Klara sent for me urgently. When I arrived at the hospital, Sister Klara, a German, spoke to me straight forward. "You are a Protestant. We need your help, but I want you to promise me you will not talk about your religion in our hospital."

I tried to surmise what this meant. Sister Klara, probably, had never spoken with a Protestant. I could imagine she had her own idea of what a Protestant was and maybe had only heard about and never met one. I had mine, and was not very attached to the concept of just sticking on a label. We all have preconceived notions about all kinds of people, and just maybe I was holding some funny ideas about nuns, even Sister Klara. After all, we do make unfounded presumptions, do we not?

"Sister Klara, this is your hospital and I will do just as you ask,"I replied with a smile. "I will not speak about my religion in your hospital." This sincere declaration was disarming. Sister Klara smiled back, satisfied. I went on to say, "Sister Klara, what is part of me is what my life is because of the one in whom I believe. I will serve you in His name." I think she was a bit perplexed, but the smiles continued.

Sister Klara had asked me to come because she expected the woman to have a difficult time child bearing. I don't remember details of the delivery of that baby, but I know I was very tired and drenched in perspiration when it was all over. It was hard work in tropical heat and no electric fan.

Sister Klara met me after the delivery with a big, warm smile. "Come, I have a cold fruit drink for you in the kitchen."

I was refreshed by the cool fruit juice she had fixed. At the table she studied me with a look that reminded me of my mother's genuine care. She said, "I didn't know that you, a Protestant pastor, could be so full of compassion."

"*Irmã* Klara, I can't speak for Protestants for that is not in my interest." I replied as gently as possible. "I am what I am because of the change Jesus made in my life."

Many were the times I was later called to help in the "Nun's Hospital." And not a few times God enabled me to show love to those who might never come to read a different book than the one of my life.

At another time and situation, Sister Klara walked the muddy track to our house to give Barbara a number intravenous solutions while a boat was sent upriver for me. Bárbara wrote about the experience in a chapter she calls, "The God Who is There."

SISTER KLARA AND THE PASTOR (again)

My dear friend, Sister Klara, took care of the bandages as they needed changing at their hospital. These courageous nuns functioned as substitutes for the then non existent doctors and cared for all of the medical responsibilities beginning with patient care and also performing all sorts of cleaning tasks.

Sister Klara sent for me. It would be another adventure into the unknown, but not unknown to the One who guided me through it all.

She informed me upon my arrival at the hospital. "We have a woman for whom midwives had delivered her baby thirteen days ago downriver."

I thought, *And...?*

Sister Klara went on to say, "The umbilical cord broke when they pulled on it."

Never! I said to myself, and then I reflected, *Never say never.*

"The placenta is still inside her. Please get it out." Dear Sister Klara, she had such faith in this pastor playing doctor.

The new sister recently arrived from Italy seemed pretty sharp. I was going to teach her to give the anesthesia while I performed a "D & C" procedure. I remembered a doctor at Hollywood Presbyterian Hospital showing me the trick of vaporizing a can of ether into a spray. If it were to drip on the face of the patient, she could experience bad reactions, even through layers of gauze.

The woman was brought in and situated on a plain metal table. I put a pin-hole in the can of ether and blew into it with all my might, held my thumb over the hole, and turned the can upside down. As I released my thumb slightly, the ether sprayed on the many layers of gauze covering the woman's face.

The Italian Sister quickly caught on how to spray the ether, and she was a success from the start. When the woman was adequately anesthetized, I proceeded to perform the "D & C." I was able to remove the placenta still lodged almost entirely in her uterus. When the woman awoke, I asked her how she felt. I never asked a person if they feel pain since that could be suggestive.

"Oh, my back hurts. This table is so hard."

Apparently the procedure was a success! The woman was thankful that her condition was treated, and that she was able to travel back downriver to her home, and no doubt continue adding to her "staircase" of kids.

Alan Bachmann

As for God, His way is perfect:
The LORD's word is flawless;
He shields all who take refuge in Him.

Psalm 18:30 (NIV)

Chapter 21: A GIRL'S FRAIL HEALTH
OPENS MANY DOORS

Our move to the village of Humaitá, which means "parakeet rocks," turned out to be a life full of surprises. (When wasn't it?) Our reputation of caring for the sick soon became known even in this new and hostile environment. One day a teenager came to consult with me. Barbara and I sat with her in one of our woven vine chairs in the front room of our old wooden house. Her name was Leonés. We had no idea who she was at the time. As it turned out, she was the only daughter of a very prominent merchant in the village. She took a big risk of incurring the wrath of the bishop for consulting with this man who, as an Evangelical, was "off limits."

She began to tell me what she was feeling. However, the story she told left out any reference to shortness of breath, light headedness, or palpitations. I could easily discern that she was extremely anemic. Her menstrual cycle was so frequent it was making her weaker. I believed that this girl was avoiding the answer to certain questions, perhaps because she believed she was tubercular. I did not mention that disease. I tried every way possible to assure her she would get better in a short time, and prescribed certain medications to that end.

When Leonés returned many weeks later, there was a vast improvement in her appearance. Her color had improved, she had gained weight and was quite exuberant. I believe she was now convinced that she had no pulmonary problems, but her treatment continued for some time. How could the town's people not see the difference in her appearance? The commentaries made the rounds.

Sometime later, this young lady married a young man whom I had treated for malaria when he was in a coma back on the Lake of the Great Snail—Uruapiára. He was completely well and worked for the municipal government in the village. A year earlier I had told Leonés that if she became pregnant she should get a full exam by a doctor in Manaus because she had a small bone structure and might have "a hard job" giving birth. Unfortunately, she didn't heed my advice.

Time passed. One day Sister Klara sent for me. "Come .It's urgent. Bring your instruments." I had no idea what was going on. When I walked into the hospital, the mayor met me and commanded, "Deliver this woman's baby!"

Yes, of course. *Humph!* Easier said than done. It would be a "nice feather in his cap" if the birth went well. When I entered the room, to my surprise it was Leonés in labor. Her father and mother had been by her bed. Her father had fainted, so he was removed from the room. Everybody seemed to be talking at once telling Leonés what to do and what not to do. It was utter confusion. I went to stand by her and whispered to her because I didn't want the others to hear and be offended. "Listen only to my voice. Tune everybody else out."

I requested help from the Italian Sister, who was called for immediately. I had to use medication to help the labor along, but I was not sure the baby could fit through Leonés' narrow birth canal. I performed an episiotomy and applied a neat little DeLee forceps (named after the father of modern obstetrics, Dr. DeLee). Soon the little gal was free to come and did so after a fashion, but for a while it was "touch and go." The Italian Sister was a great help, and we sutured up what needed to be done. The placenta came as I proceeded to knead Leonés' tummy. Fortunately there was no hemorrhaging and no postpartum infection.

Afterwards, drenched in perspiration, I went out on the front porch of the hospital overlooking the river. Leonés' father, Senhor João, was sitting there, and for some reason he looked very upset. I soon discovered why. The bishop was on the loudspeaker assailing the heretic (me) who was contaminating holy ground (in this case the hospital).

Her father was ready to go and start a fight with the bishop. Sr. João usually carried a revolver, as did many of the men in our village. Things could have gotten ugly. Sr. João told me, "I'm going to fix that man once and for all. You saved my daughter's life and my granddaughter's too. He is wrong to attack you."

"Look, do you see me battered and bleeding?" I spoke strongly to the disturbed man. "Let the bishop make all the noise he wants. He will dig himself a hole with all his raving and lose out in the end."

Sr. João calmed down and dropped the whole matter. In this culture, he would take offense at any negative remarks directed at him or any of his close friends. No one would question him if he set out to defend his honor and that of a close friend, which I now was to him.

A year or more later when the men of the congregation started the church construction, his truck carried sand up from the river and brought the bricks from the ovens where they had been baked. When they tried to settle up the bill for use of his truck, he said to the men, "As long as I live, you people will never pay for any services I can help you with."

As for God, his way is perfect:
The LORD's word is flawless;
he shields all who take refuge in him.

2 Samuel 22:31 (NIV)

Chapter 22: HOT WATER!

I was at the top of the ladder sawing one of the timbers that would be our future home. Then we could move out of the ramshackle rental we were in next to the "Post Office." (The Post Office did not handle mail, but occasionally received a telegram.)

The Doctor, recently arrived in our village, appeared below. "Hey, do you have any anesthetic?" He was not too cordial. He did not introduce himself. We had never met, and without as much as a greeting he jumped right into the question. Did I have any general anesthetics? Evidently he had heard of some activity of ours in the realm of medicine. *Uh-oh!*

"Yes," and I named two anesthetics.

"No, those won't work." Without as much as a thank you or *see you later*, he walked away.

Our conversation took place about a half mile from the hospital managed by the Sisters. He had walked in the broiling hot sun and was not in the best of moods. He'd just come from the city and his graduation from medical school in Manaus, with no residency and no internship. I thought no more about the incident except to observe that this young man had something to learn about common courtesy. His manner gave rise to the thought that perhaps he considered himself to be a bit above the level of those of us in this village, and so treated us with what appeared as disdain.

At the end of the day I walked back to our house, cleaned up with a "shower" using a bucket of water from the river. We had finished our evening meal by the light of an Aladdin Lamp. There was clapping at the door. Opening it, I was "greeted" by two men. One I knew as a very aggressive older man, known for his coarse and bossy way with people. The other man, much younger, carried a boy in his arms. The boy was partly covered with a sheet and appeared to be about nine or ten years old.

"Doctor, you're going to fix this boy up."

I hadn't even seen what there was to fix. When they uncovered his face, I was staring at a boy with one eye ready to pop out of the socket. My first thought was, *Hey there's a doctor in town, why did they come here?* So I replied, "Look, there's a doctor in town, and when there is, I do not take care of anybody, as I am only a poor substitute."

The old fellow, Romão, said, "We've been there, and he couldn't do anything for the boy." Lifting his shirt to show the 38 revolver stuck in his belt, he informed me, "You're going to do surgery on the kid and fix him up."

Barbara was standing there with me and said not a word. I am sure she was struck speechless as the scene unfolded.

Well, you don't argue much with a gun, especially when you know the one making the threat was serious. He would have no qualms about using it, and had probably done so on a number of occasions. I gave Barbara a selection of instruments to sterilize in our pressure cooker. Listening to the father and Romão, I learned of the events that led up to this moment.

Early that morning, the boy descended a log ladder from their house downriver with a knife that is used for everything from cutting up a chicken to scaling and preparing fish. Carrying the knife with the point up and towards him, he had slipped going down the log rungs, and the knife bounced in and out of the corner of the eye, severing several vital elements. The father had paddled their canoe hours to come upriver to get to our village. He had gone to the doctor and had been turned away. He was told that the repair had to be done in the big city, which was a universe away for this river dweller.

I talked to the boy about what we hoped to do. I explained that we would lay him on the table (where we had just finished our evening meal), and that I would cover his good eye so no medication might drop in it. Also he would not see what was going on. I promised to tell him what I was doing. I went in through the wound with the local anesthetic so he felt no puncture of the skin.

I checked things out in *Grey's Anatomy* before I proceeded with the repair. It was a long, tedious task. For a layman to be attempting to save a kid's eye, only the Lord could guide my hand and my brain. Finally came closure and instructions to the father about what we had done and what he should do.

Well, that was that!

Or was it? Oh, not so.

The next morning a river porter came with a verbal message that the doctor wanted to see me at the hospital. At the doctor's level of culture, I would have expected a written note rather than a verbal message.

When I stepped into his office and greeted him, he turned on me with vitriolic language, almost purple with rage. "You deceived me. You had no right to operate on that boy. He needed professional help."

"You're right," I replied in an apologetic manner. "And where is the nearest ophthalmologic surgeon? (I knew the answer, and he did too).

"Well," he said, "He would have to get a boat upriver and then a plane to Rio de Janeiro." This meant head upriver to Porto Velho and two days of flights in those days to get to Rio de Janeiro. We both knew this was the answer, but far from reality to go two days upriver then both the cost and time of a flight to Rio e Janeiro. And then schedule an appointment and surgery.

"Why did you mess with this kid's eye? I am going to have you processed and expelled from the country."

"Doctor, you will have to do what you will. I can only say we both know that with infection after twelve hours from the accident there would be no way the kid could survive in that condition for another two or three days. And the family has only a canoe and no money for this ideal solution."

He replied, "That's their problem to get to Rio de Janeiro, not mine. You wait, I'll fix you!"

The doctor appealed to the judge in town, who showed him a crown I had done on his tooth. The judge said, "Hey, leave this man alone. He has never caused a problem treating the sick or doing dentistry."

Then the doctor appealed to the mayor, who in this instance was a nice guy. The mayor called his two little daughters to come to the living room. "Look," he said to the doctor, "these two were at death's door, and that Pastor treated them, and soon they were well. You want me to condemn him?"

I am glad I didn't know that the doctor had "made the rounds" of the authorities. I left the hospital feeling low as it was. At the hospital entrance I met the Governor of Amazonas, who was in town visiting his very aged mother of whom the Sisters took care. I spoke to him about the incident with the boy and commented about the doctor's fury. I mentioned to him that I would be facing possible expulsion from Brazil for what I did to repair the boy's dislocated eye. I said, "Your Excellency, please apprise yourself of the facts. Whatever your position should be, I would highly respect your testimony in a trial."

The Governor put his arm around me and said, "Son, nobody will touch you. You saved my nephew's life." I almost folded on the spot.

Well, time heals many things. I eventually showed myself a friend to the doctor. It took a long time, but the doctor finally realized that I had no malice towards him. It was not easy for him to get over the episode, yet eventually we became cordial friends, and later he moved back to Manaus.

King Solomon, David's son wrote in one of his proverbs,

"A gentle answer turns away wrath, but a harsh word stirs up anger.

Proverbs 15:1

Chapter 23: WHITE WATER IN THE DARK

Darkness snuffs out the light of day. The sun quickly slides behind the jungle on its westward way. Clouds of mosquitoes are ready to fly in close formation on their nocturnal rampage, an open assault on any exposed flesh. I had just tied up the river launch in a safe eddy out of the current. The thirteen-foot Boston Whaler was tied to the stern of the launch. The big diesel engine was silent. Barbara could now finish getting some food cooked without risk of pots and pans rattling around and the engine's vibrations tossing it all off the stove. This was the same river port where we carried Nilo's family upriver to Humaitá. We were now on our way downriver.

Standing on the stern deck of the launch, I looked westward at the retreating light. All of a sudden, a huge tug boat came into view from downriver. I recognized the river pilot. "Tiradentes" (*tooth puller*) was a friend and one of the best on the river to navigate larger craft. He had been contracted to guide the huge tug on this treacherous river. The Captain of any vessel has to trust men like Tiradentes. The river pilot knew the river like the palm of his hand. His nickname was given in honor of the courageous Joaquim da Silva Xavier, the hero of Brazil in the 1792 struggle for independence—generations ago, nothing to do with teeth.

When Tiradentes recognized me, he waived. I thought, *There they go.* But the tug slowed out there in the main channel. With the tug engine idling, just holding forward against the strong current, my voice could be heard. "What's up?"

"We have an oil tanker stuck on rocks upriver. She's taking on water and the river level is dropping. We have a huge pump to get the water out and float her off the rocks."

I shouted back: "Good luck!" But that didn't end things.

The river pilot called out and asked, "Can you help us? We can't run this part of the river at night. It's too dangerous, but you could take this pump in your boat with its powerful outboard and get there real fast. I'll go with you."

No way out of this one. I hoped the next line would be my best one. "I need gasoline and oil for my 50 HP Mercury."

Almost immediately, a deck hand pushed over a fifty gallon drum of gasoline and a five gallon can of oil. I only needed ten gallons of gasoline and five quarts of oil. Wow! What a surplus! I dove in and swam the drum of gasoline and can of oil to shore. I made short work of fueling my tank in the whaler.

I told Barbara I was going to run upriver. What a wife God gave me. Barbara never questioned some of the risky things I got myself into.

The tug was holding against the river current out in the main channel. I went out in the whaler and Tiradentes climbed on board. I sat at the bench with steering and remote controls to the Mercury motor, and he sat beside me.

Off we went with no spotlight. You can see the river outline best in darkness anyhow. It's not so much knowing where all the rocks, sandbars and logs are, but to know where they are not. Just know the channel and keep to where the dangers are not. A little bit like life itself?

About an hour out, we had to cut sharply left across the river where the channel went between two huge underwater parallel ledges of rock that stretched from one side almost to the other side of the river. Here the current surged and churned.

We were bouncing around in some rough current when Tiradentes asked, "Where are Baiano's Rocks?"

"We just passed between them," I shouted above the din of the outboard motor. He let out a loud whoop. I couldn't tell if he was scared, surprised, or what. The rocks were named for the worst remembered river disaster that occurred here.

Not long after, with a few maneuvers to follow channels, we pulled up alongside the oil tanker. Rapidly they off-loaded the pump. I tied up the whaler and went on board. The cook offered me a luscious meal of bacon, eggs, and some high class meat which he fixed for me, a hungry river man, not used to such fare. He watched me devour everything on my plate. Plenty of hot coffee filtered down through my very full stomach. The clock announced that it was already an hour past midnight.

It was time for me to return downriver to where my family waited. I called to Tiradentes, friend and river pilot, to ride with me back to the waiting tugboat. He told me I was nuts, and said he would wait for the tug, which in daylight would come safely on upriver.

I returned to my family on the launch. At dawn I cranked up its diesel engine and we headed downriver to the village of Manicore, towing the whaler on the stern.

My God made the universe. He is all powerful to watch over little me in the face of any danger and He always has.

But the eyes of the LORD are on those who fear him, on those whose hope is in his unfailing love.

Psalm 33:18

Chapter 24: SHOW-DOWN ON THE BAND STAND

When we moved to this village of 800, much was the speculation as to why such a family would come live here. Hiding? Climbing the ladder of success?

One day early on, I received a visit from a rather big and cumbersome oaf who came to our rickety wooden rental house. He was quite aggressive in his attitude. No sooner had I invited him in and he had seated himself in one of our vine chairs than he charged forth with his interrogation. His name was "Juca," a nickname that seemed to fit.

"What are you doing here?" Juca asked.

"What did he mean by 'here?'" I replied with what I hoped was a disarming smile. "Why, I am here talking with you."

That threw him off.

I asked, "And what are you doing here?" (The implication was, Why did you come here?) He claimed to represent the Sons of Mary and implied that I owed them an explanation.

At the end of it all, I told him we had been sent here.

He never asked who had sent us, to which I would have replied that God had sent us to show and tell all we could of His love for sinners and His offer of forgiveness and salvation to life eternal to all who would trust in Him. The up-shot of this encounter left Juca rather confused to think things through and perhaps develop a new "response mechanism" to deal with this pastor. Juca could not make out why we would come to such a remote village, supposing that with our learning and ways to serve, he expected that we should be looking for a "Place in the Sun" that would feed our egos and start us on the climb up the status ladder of society. We didn't fit any of Juca's presuppositions, least of all belonging to the "right religion."

Time passed. An event occurred on the little band stand on the town square that I would only learn about years later.

Now we must back track to an earlier moment. One time on a trip upriver in the big thirty-six-foot mission diesel launch, when Barbara was along with our three kids, we stopped at a river port about two days downriver from our destination of Humaitá. Barbara and I and our kids were living on board the mission river launch as we travelled. With its powerful diesel engine, I towed a second boat alongside in which, free of the vibrations and noise, she could cook as we chugged upriver. She would settle the kids in their hammocks after the noon meal. We didn't travel at night as the considerable risk of numerous dangers made it imprudent to travel the treacherous Madeira River at night with a family.

At this river port I relate "White Water in the Dark," an experience that took place there. Our launch was secure. We were tied up for the night. A lady with two little girls asked for passage to Humaitá where her husband had found a job. Normally it is very complicated to carry others in one's launch. Both Barbara and I felt there was no other option. Because we were a family, it was both safe and acceptable to accommodate this woman and her two small children. There would be a few more to feed and more hammocks to hang. Part of river culture.

Arriving in Humaitá, the lady thanked us and asked, "How much did that cost?" This is a custom which anticipates a reply that rejects any thought of payment, yet it shows gratitude for the value of the help given. That seemed to be the end of the episode. In Humaitá we took up residence and among other events, met up with a visit from Juca.

Little did I know to whom this woman was espoused. He was a very violent truck driver working on the dirt track across this segment of the Amazon, later called the "Trans Amazon Highway".

Nilo Costa was known for taking no guff from anyone and kept a 38 revolver by his side on the seat of the vehicle he drove. The phrase "he had no hair on his tongue" was used to describe a person of quick reaction. He was a person of direct and decisive speech, who was not prone to the diplomacy of a gentler manner of talk. In Humaitá we had never exchanged so much as a word, but apparently he was much aware of the favor we did him by bringing his wife and kiddies from downriver.

It was some years later in the city of Manaus that I observed a man step down from the cab of a cattle truck. It was Nilo. I greeted him with, "Nilo Costa, Humaitá, Street of the Flowers," and mentioned the year.

His reply opened a box of mystery. "You knew my name. You remember me from Humaitá? Now I know I did the right thing way back then with Juca and his gang."

"Oh, what was that?" I responded.

Nilo told me of a Sunday afternoon he was seated in the covered band stand (no band used it). Juca and his cronies were fooling around the band stand, and all of a sudden they got the wild idea to go to the house of the missionary pastor and give him a good "going over." After all, he was an Evangelical, so not of our "faith."

When these rabble rousers got up to leave, Nilo pulled his 38 revolver out of his belt and said, "Okay, you jerks, just sit down and cool off. You're going nowhere, and you're not going to mess with the Pastor."

I am sure they knew Nilo would use the gun. And so Nilo went on to tell me that the rabble rousers lost all enthusiasm to "bust up" the Pastor. Never again did they try that one.

What was it that made Nilo feel a concern to protect us? Maybe I should ask , "Who?" God can use even the wrath of men to praise Him.

*"You will go on your way in safety
and your foot will not stumble."*

King Solomon, in Proverbs 3:23 NIV

Chapter 25: THE TIME OF OUR LIFE

It's the question that begs everyday of our lives. Our time and how we spend it. How do we use this fleeting gift measured out one day at a time? This thought jumped out at me, living among people who told time by sun and stars.

The river culture of Amazonas has its unique way of looking at each day. River and lake dwellers depend on ingenuity to survive the harsh life of their habitat. Each river launch that comes along is heard long before it appears. These folk learn to know the peculiar sound of the engine of each riverboat. Whether it is a river trader or a passenger boat plying the currents and bends of the river, they will know who it is.

Our big diesel launch was well known on the Madeira River. Each one that chugs up and down the estimated 1,300 miles of river is recognized by its sound as well as the silhouette of the superstructure outlined on the water. It tells the river and lake dweller much.

We were on the upper reaches of the Madeira River, navigating our way downriver to a plantation where many would be waiting for medical and dental attention. It was yet early in the morning. We had been under way since dawn. Just a bend above our destination, a group of people stood on the river bank, one waving a white cloth, the generally accepted call for help, or at least a stop. We swung the launch around in a wide circle to pull into the river bank heading up against the current for better control of the launch as we came in to tie up.

My heart sank. What a pathetic looking group of sickly, poorly clothed and undernourished ones of God's creation. And of His love? It was unknown to them. Much was so immediately visible. Kids with conjunctivitis, eyes closed, pus gluing them shut. Mothers with a staircase of kids, the littlest one on the breast, another in the tummy. Where to start? And all the while remembering we had a promise to keep at the plantation just beyond the next bend in the river. Time! There's never enough of it.

Yes, it takes more than a moment to dispense medication with a healthy dose of comments about hygiene and nutrition added in. If we didn't care, where would they find what they needed? Living as they do on a barter system, how would they pay for it? I thought back to another world when I wrote "Dreams Grow Feet," (Chapter 3) before I could yet know what God was steering us into.

Look at them. Did you ever see such a sorry lot? I had seen and would see many more. I never got over the anguish I felt every time I saw the misery, the hopelessness on their faces. Only the compassion of Christ moves us to do more than wring our hands in lament.

Food to nourish was a priority, but sickly people are often too frail, too lethargic to fend for themselves. They lack the know-how and motivation to provide well for their own needs. Time. The time ticks on as we talk with them.

I built stories to put into terms they can understand the lessons they will remember about hygiene, cleanliness of their own bodies and of their children and good nutrition from what is available. Two Brazil nuts have the same protein as that of one chicken egg. A local palm fruit, Açaí (ah-sah-ee) is very high in iron. Another, Tucumã (too-koo-mah) is rich in vitamin A. The papaya fruit is highly nutritious and the seeds are a first line for eradication of the intestinal parasite, a round worm we call *lumbriga*. And so a story weaves these elements in, not always with very scientific basis. I talk about this in the chapter "Miracle Milk" on Great Snail Lake.

Time was getting away from us. The sun had reached the top of its travel across the sky. The folk downriver were waiting. We finally cranked up the diesel launch and were soon under way. As we came into view of the plantation, the riverbank was covered with people. They had been waiting since dawn but had not lost hope that somehow we would keep our word. What patience hope builds when people so abused by empty promises trust in your word. One's reputation is made or broken on that one point. As Christ's ambassador, what I am is the imperative. People only see that by my attitude and action. A preacher of a bygone era, Dwight L. Moody, said, "If I take care of my character (what I am) my reputation will take care of itself."

Greetings were made all around with our most humble apologies for being so late to arrive. Soon we were at it. I most always travelled with a companion to help run and care for the launch and help with the paraphernalia involved to care for people.

When I scooted from place to place in my fast outboard, I usually went alone or one of my kids came along as home was close by— never more than a couple of hours away by river from our jungle house on the lake.

Very soon I had sorted out the dental problems from the other needs of this gathering. Once I had done the nerve blocks with Novocain injections on a few mouths, I began to consult with others about their illnesses. While setting up, I had listened to the conversations all around. People would be comparing their illnesses with each other. When I put a stethoscope to their heart and lungs or sphygmomanometer (blood pressure cuff) on their arm, they would be so entranced with the attention I gave them that they often forgot to tell me of certain symptoms they felt. Having listened to a lot of the chatter earlier, I could insert questions until we got to the bottom of the cause: anemia, intestinal parasites, malaria, and sometimes Hansen's disease (leprosy) or leishmaniasis (cutaneous) bacterial infection or some other ailment common among the river people.

Once they see the "bugs" through the microscope,
teaching hygiene is easier.

Conversation continued with one and then another while I was
extracting teeth. This type of "open forum" was also profitable as I
would explain to one the cause of what they were experiencing. Others
would later recall something I said about hygiene or nutrition and
"steal" the idea and take it home in their memory. Oral culture people
(often unable to read or write) rely on their highly developed and very
good memory. They do not need to take notes on everything like we of
a literate and linear culture do.

By about 8:30 pm we were done and "done in." We sat at table
with those in charge of the plantation, which included the owner's
wife. We hadn't eaten all day so we really "put it away"—several
types of game, fish, and manioc meal led the menu. While we
concentrated on the food, the lady of the house said, "You know, back
on the lake lives a lady so sick that she couldn't come. I promised her I
would ask you to go see her. Will you?"

We didn't know what we were getting into, but we said, "Yes,
we'll go see her. Can someone take us by canoe?"

We soon found out what we had said yes to. About 9:30 pm, a young fellow led us to the canoe. A smoky, yellow, open-wick kerosene lamp—*lamparina*—led our way to the dugout canoe. We sloshed barefoot through a swamp in muck nearly up to our knees to get to the canoe.

We asked the fellow who paddled the dugout, "Is it far?"

He answered that it was just across the lake "a little ways." About an hour and a half later, we arrived at a little palm house. We called, "Hello the house." Soon we saw a light—that yellow, open wick *lamparina*.

I had brought along a flashlight and some medication. We had no idea what we'd find. Not only was the woman in a destitute situation partially from neglect, and also one of her children was very sick.

I carried a selection of medicines not normally available on a passing river trader or at some plantation. What I knew was available locally, I prescribed. The dear lady did her best to host us with a brew of home-ground coffee and manioc-meal biscuits.

Other people began to arrive. The "jungle-vine radio" is amazingly fast. Medication given and the instructions repeated back orally gave us the hope that they would follow through with what I recommended. There were those who had such hope in hearing a word from the "doctor" that they would say, "Just bless a cup of water for me and I'll be well." I am sure that the compassion of Christ shows through. His compassion is seen through us, and it makes all the difference. God touches people.

The stars told us it was time to go. We traversed the lake, the swamp, got on board, and "fired-up" the diesel. A pink sky announced a new day. No sleep now, but we were soon underway with the hopes of respite in a hammock for at least a little while as time chased us on downriver. Yes, we were spending the time of our lives. One more day had ticked away. What did this new day hold for us?

Give praise to the LORD, proclaim his name;
make known among the nations what he has done.

King David, in I Chronicles 16:8 NIV

Chapter 26: A PAUSE, WALKING TO CHURCH

We were walking down the dirt track along the river on our way to church where we met Sundays in a large palm thatch house. As I passed the rather worn down palm house of Senhor Miguel, he was standing there leaning against the palm thatch wall with a home-made cigarette hanging from the corner of his mouth. He looked so laid back like he had not a care in the world.

"And how is your wife today?" I asked.

"She's trying to have a baby. There's a midwife there with her."

"Can I help or, is everything Okay?"

He suggested that I go in to see what I could do.

I helped the midwife get out two little guys and told her to wait for the placenta. After church I was walking home and as I passed Sr. Miguel's palm thatch, there he stood as if he hadn't moved.

"How is your wife doing?"

"It's hard to say. The midwife couldn't figure out what's happening." The midwife had gone home.

"Should I go in?" I asked.

"Go ahead," he said.

Without telling some of the details, we got number three out and two placentas. She had identical twins and a second pregnancy with its own placenta.

Several days later it became apparent that one of the babies had a focus of infection on the corner of his jaw. I learned that a doctor was in the village, so I asked him if he would come and open this pustule and treat it. His reply was to say he didn't have any surgical instruments with him. I offered him the use of my surgical instruments.

"No," he said, "I wouldn't be accustomed to your instruments."

What? Instruments are quite universal, so a Kelly curved or straight, an Allis, etc. Names may alter but it's the hands that matter. So guess who did surgery on this five-day-old baby?

The father, Senhor Miguel, asked me to take a picture of him holding the three newborns. I didn't walk around with a camera. It was anti-culture, but I got mine, took the photo and developed it in my "dark room" (kitchen sink at night) and gave him a black and white print of the negative I had developed.

Perhaps three weeks went by when a passing river trader stopped in our village and left a newspaper from the city of Manaus. It had a picture of Sr. Miguel and his three boys, described as triplets. The article stated that Dr. "What's his name" had delivered the three.

When the news got around the village, the dear man was so demoralized by the lie that he left town. I never said a word. He fixed things up all by himself! The report he wrote to the newspaper helped him put his foot in his mouth.

There's no limit to what you can do if you don't care who gets the applause.

COULD A MOTHER BEAR SIX BABIES TO LOSE EACH AT BIRTH?

A woman came for a consultation. She was distressed. She had given birth to six babies. All died as they were being born at the hands of a midwife. The mother was quite deaf, perhaps from measles as a child, but we could communicate. She lived in a most simple two-room wood frame excuse for a house. Her husband, indifferent to her plight, had certainly given her six pregnancies. Stoic as they were, you either "make it" or you don't.

At the end of the consultation, I promised this dear lady that I would deliver her next child if she should happen to become pregnant. (She probably already was. Why else would she have come?) I asked her to keep me advised. In due time, she sent for me. I went to this little house to be with her throughout labor. As the head presented itself, it was still encapsulated in the "bag of water." I quickly surmised that her previous six babies had literally drowned once out of the birth canal.

I readied a plastic basin and placed a blunt scissor over my fingers, but not in the loops. I snipped the membrane, tossed the scissors and caught the baby. The little guy cried loudly and was full of life. The woman was so joyful. Even she could hear the little one cry. Tears blurred my vision.

How many babies could be saved if only there was just a bit of knowledge and a measure of compassion?

MIDWIVES STEAL A SECRET FROM ME

There was a period in our career when confidence in my medical experience placed me in a number of "no way out situations." This was true for a time with midwives. Often they had "tried everything" and could not get the baby to make its appearance into the world. The mother might very well suffer exceedingly to no avail. When things got to what looked like the "point of no return," a midwife would come after me or someone would send for me. Sometimes the delivery presented an arm first, sometimes a leg, and on occasion it was a breech birth (rear end first).

I had seen the scenario enough times to hope for the better, but expect the worst. The mother to be would be sitting on a wooden box or be flat out on a mat. The local "tools" usually consisted of some old gals with their pipes or chewing tobacco and a pair of rusty scissors used for everything for which scissors could be used. To check the baby's decent they had a sardine can full of pig fat. They also had a piece of thin string to tie off the umbilical cord and some old cloths that would clean up (?) the mother after the little guy or gal put in its appearance. Then they would leave mother and baby to go bury the placenta at the base of a tree.

When I appeared, I would come with a few items that these old gals could get together themselves with a little forethought and creativity. I had a pair of blunt-nosed stainless steel scissors, pre-sterilized glass hypodermics, a thick piece of string, a number of cloth diapers, a cookie sheet, a squirt-bottle of alcohol, and matches. On sight I would ask someone to run the charcoal iron over the diapers. This also gave the midwives one more silent lesson in cleanliness.

The art of the theatricals of the event, if I were in charge, was to wash the mother in this area, wash my own hands, and nevermore touch anything until the baby would come. On occasion an injection would help the dear tired mother push the baby on out.

Catching the baby, I would hold him lower than the mother if she were sitting on a box or the edge of a hammock. Summarily I would "milk" the blood from the umbilical cord to the baby and only then tie it off with a thick string. After I cleaned the baby up, I would give her to the mother to hold and nurse. The uterus would start closing down. Kneading the tummy, I could help free the placenta so it would eventually be expelled. Never should one pull on the umbilical cord coming from the placenta. But that's what the midwives often did.

The midwives observed me on a number of these situations and probably had some conversations about the way I did things. I never criticized them. On a given occasion, one of the midwives came to get me to help with the birth by a young woman. It would be her first baby, and the midwives seemed quite preoccupied. When she asked me to help I replied that they very well knew how to deliver babies, so why should I go? She surprised me with her response. "We have discovered your secret. You have holy hands!"

I had no idea what she was talking about. If I asked what she meant, she would reply, Oh, you know. The way I found out what she meant was by asking, "How did you discover my secret?"

She went on to explain that they had been watching me and my every move. "You don't use pig grease. You flame any instrument you use and they are all so shiny. You milk the blood in the placental cord to the baby.

"Your babies are always so pink and lively and nurse so well. Another thing: you never pull on the placental cord. Rather, you massage the mother's tummy until the placenta pops out."

I gave a groan to accentuate the importance of her discovery, and asked her not to tell anyone about my secret. Exactly! She probably told all the other midwives, and the news spread up and down the river. The leak of the "secret" changed the way many midwives delivered babies.

"Knowledge applied is wisdom.
God given wisdom.
To function in their world,
The midwives believed I had the former.
They learned and gained from the latter."

"...for gaining wisdom and instruction; for understanding words of insight..."

Proverbs 1:2

Chapter 27: WHAT DOES AN ANGEL LOOK LIKE?

The two wooden panels called "windows" opened onto our front porch under the tin roof that covered it. No glass. No screen. I looked out over the river. The rain was torrential. I felt like I was standing behind a water fall. All details were lost in the blur of the downpour. It obliterated the other side of the mighty Madeira River a half mile away. The dirt track between our house and the river bluff was a quagmire of red clay. Rain that began before dawn usually took all day to run its course, and may go on into the night.

How cozy and dry I felt in this new board house. I had just finished building with the logs from the jungle which were hand-sawed into boards and beams. Cozy was a feeling to be short-lived.

I first heard the sound of the tractor as it came into view out of the gloom. It was pulling a four-wheel cart. Lauro, deacon of the just-beginning congregation, waved to me from under his straw hat. He looked to be soaked to the skin. The tractor lurched to a stop in the greasy red clay we called "our road." We met under the tin roof of the porch area just inside the gate. The rain hammering the corrugated tin over the porch was deafening.

"Lauro, please repeat. I can hardly hear you." The story quickly unfolded. A little guy called an Arigô–"The Wanderer"—had passed along a trail way back in the dense jungle and had come upon Raymond and his family in a simple palm shelter. The "wanderer" trekked through the night and nearly fifty miles of jungle–reptiles, jaguars and all—to bring us this urgent news. The "Wanderer" told Lauro that Raymond recognized no one. He was speaking to no one, not even his wife. The "Wanderer" begged us to go rescue Raymond. Strangely, nobody ever again saw this "Arigô" around the village or could say where he went.

Our brother Raymond was in a dire situation, many hours away in the jungle in a palm thatch shelter with his wife and kiddies. Lauro asked, "Will you go with me?"

With my "yes" answer and a word to my wife Barbara, I grabbed my shotgun and off we went. Or, should I say, we churned away through the sticky red clay that passed in front of our house. It was close on to three o'clock in the afternoon.

I stood behind Lauro on the tractor-hitch bar. Literally I rode "shotgun"–a double barrel that I kept at the ready throughout the long trip. And the rain came down and down. The one headlight of the tractor fought its way through the rain and heavy jungle foliage. Twice we crossed swollen watercourses on "bridges" made of only two slippery logs that others had felled on some previous travel over this jungle track.

We safely crossed two of these and finally arrived nine hours later at a little palm-thatch shelter just next to another watercourse. It was midnight. Finally the rain was letting up. Nine wet and dreary hours now separated us from our village.

There stood Raymond under the palm thatch. No greeting. He said not a word. He seemed so disconnected. So passive. I have heard it described as "spaced out."

What was Raymond doing so far back in the jungle? He was extracting sap, a "milk" from the Sorva tree, a product basic to certain hospital supplies and for chewing gum. His harvest process was to build a scaffold of wooden poles lashed together with the right kind of vine. He then climbed the tree and from the scaffold, scored the trunk in long, zig-zag diagonal grooves down the tree. At the base the "milk" was collected into square five gallon cans. After heating this sap/milk to a certain point over an open fire, a solid white block resulted. It was then removed from the square can and the *"balata"* became more easily transportable.

Often with water up to his neck, Raymond floated the blocks of *balata* along this watercourse to this palm thatched shelter where his wife and children stayed. In this humble home they cooked what the jungle provided and slept in hammocks under mosquito nets. There he stored the blocks of *balata* until they could be brought to market in our village at the edge of the Madeira River. A trader boat would buy this and off it would go to somewhere in the world.

I wondered if a vampire bat or some unknown "exotic" creature had bitten him along this waterway. In the Amazon we only have alligators and no crocodiles. Yet if he had met up with an alligator, we would not have seen Raymond ever again.

Pots, dishes, sacks with hammocks, we loaded all into the cart behind the tractor along with mosquito nets, the kids, his wife, and Raymond. We placed him on a cot I had rigged. It would ease the teeth-jarring ride for Raymond, even if not so for his wife and kids.

I tried to examine Raymond, but I was at a loss to discover any indication of a health problem. An hour after arriving, we started out. The rain became a drizzle. By 1 am we were on our way back to our village. It was slower going with care of the family in the cart. We arrived the following afternoon, twenty-four hours from the outset. We decided to take Raymond right to the little hospital run by some local nuns. No professional medical staff existed. "Hospital" in this context was a boarding house for the sick. The then-current perspective of the populace was that if you went to the hospital you probably were too ill to ever leave (except in a coffin). The hospital also served for some difficult birth situations.

We had a cordial relationship with the "sisters." After a test case or two, they trusted me enough to call me in to their hospital to handle some of the very complicated births and other situations.

It was late Thursday afternoon when we left Raymond at the hospital. Later in the week, Sister Klara, an elderly German nun, reported that there were no noticeable signs of change through Saturday. The little congregation of believers prayed for Raymond in their homes throughout these days. Sunday morning about 8:30, we gathered in the modest palm-thatch house where we met. Just as we began to sing a hymn, low and behold, who comes up the wooden steps to greet us? Raymond! He greeted everyone in the Name of Our Lord and seated himself on one of the board planks that comprised the furniture of our place of worship.

Did God intervene? Later, Sister Klara told us that at a given moment early Sunday morning, Raymond got out of the hospital bed, showered, shaved and got dressed. The sister asked, "And where are you going?"

"I am going to worship my Lord and Savior." For the first time, Raymond spoke to sister Klara."It's time to go."

The whole village heard by the "jungle vine" the story of Arigô, this little fellow, "The Wanderer," bringing the news of Raymond's condition. The story of our trek back in the jungle through the night to rescue Raymond was making the rounds, even up and down the river. After the Arigô informed Senhor Lauro about the sad state of affairs of Raymond this Arigô was never again seen or heard from by anyone.

Is that what an angel looks like?

Raymond had been given up by the community as a hopeless "basket case." And what did the Sisters at the hospital think? Who knows? In all the saga there was only one real "But…"But God— whose hand of blessing and watch-care demonstrated to those who do follow Him and to skeptics as well that He, our God, is all powerful His wonders to perform, the skeptic and unbelieving man to confuse and confound.

"Lead me in a straight path."

A Psalm of King David, Psalm 27:11a (NIV)

Chapter 28: WALKING ON EGGS

Time moved along in this village. A young couple in our small congregation wanted to marry. We had no place where we could hold a wedding since we were meeting in a palm thatch house. I went to the mayor, Senhor Joseph, who had become our friend, and asked him about the possibility of using the Municipal Hall. He readily consented and offered to give away the bride since her parents lived many days downriver and would be unable to attend. I wrote up the wedding papers as this would be a "religious wedding with civil effect." Actually, it would be the first legal wedding in this municipality in many years. Most men married one woman in a religious ceremony (which had no legal status) and married another woman (elsewhere) in a civil ceremony in that city or town.

There was a judge in town. I invited him to preside over the legal part and the signing of the papers to be filed with the government. He graciously agreed to do this. The reception would be held in our wood frame house, which I had recently finished building. Leonés, whose delivery I had performed in the hospital, daughter to the merchant John, went to our house and scrubbed the floors.

On the eve of the wedding, I was walking across the little town square and there in the cool of the evening sat the Judge. "Good evening, Your Honor. Everything is ready for tomorrow."

"There will be no wedding, and I will not officiate," he replied.

You could have knocked me over with a feather. All I could say was, "Oh," and I walked away. I went to find the mayor and told him the news.

"Wait a minute," he huffed. "Who is the mayor here, and who gives the orders for the use of the town hall? And after all, I am going to give away the bride." So, all systems were go, judge or not!

The Municipal Hall and all of the offices were on the floor above street level. The area underneath, at ground level, was closed in for storage. A man who made straw mattresses kept his select pile of straw in that area near one of the entrances to this storage area. Since he suspected some of the straw was being stolen, he had a fellow sleep on that pile of straw. The judge's apartment was upstairs next to his chambers. The fellow watching the straw noticed that almost nightly, a woman would slip in late in the evening and go to the judge's room. The bishop apparently was also aware of what was going on. I later learned the story.

Dom Michael went to the judge as if to save him from vile "rumors" of different women spending the night with him. The bishop named the women and the hour when they came and went, describing the "rumor" in such a way that the judge knew that the bishop held the evidence. The judge's secret was out. The appeal by the bishop appeared as if wishing to "protect" the judge from these terrible rumors.

"What if your wife in Manaus should hear of this?" the bishop subtly inferred. In exchange for the bishop's silence, he suggested that the judge should not get involved in the wedding of these two evangelicals. For that reason, on the eve of the wedding, "His Honor" (without honor) told me that night on the town square that there would be no wedding.

I could readily see that I could end up in the middle of all this. I had no idea that the judge and the bishop had reached an "understanding." Something was afoot to break up this wedding. The ceremony was scheduled for two o'clock the next day.

I kept all this information to myself and realized I needed wisdom I didn't have. Only the Lord could show me how to walk through political nuances of this small town. God alerted me to something I had not thought about. I stopped by the police office—a little cubicle with a man in uniform supposedly there to keep law and order. He had two guards, each uniformed and armed with World War I rifles that looked okay but wouldn't fire a bullet if they had to. I apologized for not sending them a written invitation to attend the wedding, but asked if they would please stand at the door to the hall and allow entrance only to families but to no children not accompanied by their parents.

The policeman and his two guards were very excited to be shown such prestige. That day my suspicions were confirmed. A bunch of kids had been recruited to invade the wedding ceremony and cause pandemonium. My police friends never let them near the door.

The Mayor and I had a good time and the day's events were not disrupted at all. The reception came off without a hitch. The three-layer wedding cake baked by Leonés was the talk of the town.

If any of you lacks wisdom, you should ask God, who gives generously to all without finding fault, and it will be given to you.

James, brother of Jesus, in James 1:5 (NIV)

Chapter 29: THE PRIEST AND THE PASTOR

I had gone upriver with another pastor in my fifty horsepower
Mercury outboard on a Boston whaler, the safest combination to run
the treacherous Madeira River. The village where we stopped
separated two regions. Years ago this place was a collection center for
rubber. The name Calama ended up being called "Calamity" because
of the economic decadence. The village had become the habitat of
fisherman and their families. Pastor Darciso had asked me to leave him
here in Calama. He hoped to catch a ride home on a fishing boat
heading upriver for a journey of two or three days to Porto Velho, or
longer if they did fishing on the way!

One way to connect all these remote little places through the
Amazon was to listen to the radio messages from people in the city at
either end of the river, in Porto Velho, or in Manaus. For a few cents, a
message was read so that folks back home in some port or plantation
would hear news of their friend or relative in the city. It could be news
of their travel home; treatment in a hospital; sending for a person to
come to the city; the price of produce extracted from the jungle; or a
letter or package being sent along on some riverboat that was going to
pass that way.

In this village, we found an abandoned house of a rich rubber
trader of yesteryear. Pastor Darciso and I hung our hammocks in a big
room nearest to any breeze off the river. We didn't have mosquito
nets, so we had to swing in our hammocks to give the hungry
mosquitoes a chase to zap us. Along about midnight, Pastor Darciso
had a brilliant idea. "If I could find gasoline and oil to mix for the

outboard somewhere in the village, would you take me to Porto Velho?" It would be at least a fast and wild eight hours or so on the river, depending upon rain or shine.

I was so sure he wouldn't find twenty-five gallons of gasoline that I agreed to his ludicrous proposal. By a rare chance, somebody may have some stored in a steel barrel. And then he'd have to find oil to mix with the gasoline. So I agreed that *if* he found the gasoline and the oil, I would run him up to Porto Velho. By the way, I would be gone two more days, and my wife wouldn't know why I hadn't come back the day after I left.

Almost an hour after midnight, Pastor Darciso came in wearing a big grin. "I got the gas and oil."

Over the radio came the messages from folk in the city being read on the air telling those along the river of all sorts of happenings such as the current illness treated, prices of rubber somebody sold or Brazil nuts, and whatever they wanted sent on the next boat up or downriver. One message was a request by the bishop in Porto Velho for the local priest to come to Porto Velho from Calama, the town from which Pastor Darciso wanted me to take him.

By dawn, with the resourcefulness of my colleague, Darciso, some coffee and manioc cakes appeared. As we ate, there was a clapping in the doorway—where a door no longer hung. As I turned, I was face to face with the priest's altar boy. By way of the radio messages, the bishop had sent one requesting the priest in this village of Calama to get to Porto Velho as soon as possible. So the task of the altar boy was to ask if we would take the priest with us. Even though Pastor Darciso had located the gasoline and oil a little after midnight, nothing escaped the ever probing eye of the local priest.

Rather than return a verbal reply, I considered the "second mile" Jesus talked about. I told the boy that I would go see the priest myself. I could easily reply a verbal no, but speaking with the priest would be a more respectful communication.

When the boy left, I told Darciso that I was afraid the weight of three of us and extra cans of gasoline would be too much for the boat to get up on a "plane" and skip along on top of the water. If it only plowed along, the whole purpose of speed would be defeated.

I went out to look for the priest. As I neared the chapel, I saw Padre Romano. He was well known for his tenacity and dedication as a priest. Often he travelled rivers and lakes to be present at various saint's day celebrations. When the party got out of hand and drink dominated revelers, the priest frequently became the brunt of some bad humor.

As I approached Padre Romano, he looked neat in his black hat and habit and was just about to hold mass in the little old wooden Chapel. I greeted him. His response was one of apparent mixed emotions. For years he felt very unhappy with me because of what he understood that I believed. He was sincere in his opposition, but I wished I could clarify some things. In the end, my example would say more than words. I asked Padre Romano when he would be finished administering the mass and set a departure time.

By 7:30 we had the fuel on board and were ready to leave. Padre Romano arrived at river's edge in his white and well worn work habit. He was a bit nervous. He didn't know how to swim, and he was at the mercy of the man he thought of as the opposition. The river was like glass, which meant it would be hard for the hull to come unglued from the water's slick surface. I was about to think we weren't going to get the boat up on a plane.

Moving out from the shore, a blast of wind came out of nowhere to ripple the surface of the river. I gunned the engine. Wow! The hull broke loose we got up on a plane and moved out. As the fuel burned, we would become lighter by the hour

Around noon, we were coming up on St. Carlos, a well known plantation for rubber, Brazil nuts and other products from the jungle. Pastor Darciso knew a family here, believers in Jesus who had moved to this plantation from his church in the city. We would stop for a short rest and hope they could rustle up some fish and rice.

Padre Romano was at a loss how to look at all this. He had never been so near followers of Jesus and so outside his purveyance. As we sat down to the rickety table—the split palm log floor—our host gave us a bountiful and delicious meal administered with love and care. Pastor Darciso, in giving thanks for the sumptuous meal, thanked the Lord for safe travel and asked God's continued protection on Padre Romano and us.

With a good meal of fish and manioc powder to take with us, and with plenty of water from the river, we were ready to go. I was first to return to the river and dove under the boat to see if anything had punched any dents in the fiberglass hull.

When I came to the surface, Padre Romano stared into the water, very pensive.

"Padre Romano, how are you doing?" I asked. "Are you being well cared for? Ready to travel?"

"You people have shown me love and care more than my people." His remark was rather emotional. The trip for the next four or five hours was safe and uneventful on to Porto Velho.

After this experience, Padre Romano became a respected friend and would greet me whenever he spotted me on a village street or somewhere along the river.

We are told to love those who persecute us for Jesus' sake and turn the other side of our face. When we show His love to folk like Padre Romano, only blessings can result. They do and they did.

But I tell you, love your enemies and pray for those who persecute you, that you may be children of your Father in heaven.

Matthew 5:44, 45a (NIV

Chapter 30: INDIFFERENCE MAKES NO
DIFFERENCE

From the Madeira River I trotted over a jungle trail at a rapid pace for twenty minutes or so to a canoe left for me at one end of Lake Matopiri. As always, my backpack included an assortment of emergency surgical instruments. Arriving at the canoe, I found the paddle stuck in the brush out of the sun. Soon I was on my way to paddle across the lake to the other end, where I would meet with the congregation.

I wasn't far along when I was being called by a white cloth to a port on the lake. The rise and fall of the level meant that most houses were some way up the trail safe from high water. I turned into the port, tied up the canoe and started up the trail. Coming towards me was a robust man carrying a casting net on the paddle resting on his shoulder and in the other hand a seven foot long harpoon to throw at the big Pirarucu fish. As he passed with a murmur, he showed no expression of greeting. He was just a person passing on the trail.

A little way up the path I came to the house. A person invited me in. They were all quite solemn. I couldn't figure what was going on. They brought me into the room, hot, muggy and poorly ventilated. The palm thatch "windows" were not propped open as was the normal situation when there was no wind-blown rain. There sat a rather young woman in the agony of excruciating pain. Both her breasts had massive infections. The cause and onset were now not very relevant. What to do?

This woman would only find relief if I opened both breasts in the right place and manner. Local anesthetic would only spread the infection and be of no use in the affected areas. With what resources were at hand, I got out my scalpel, washed my hands and the surfaces, and made some radical, deep, defined incisions in one and then the other breast. What a mess! But relief was instant. After the initial dressing and more instructions as to care and cleanliness, I started packing out. I left antibiotics, knowing that there's always someone who knows how to use a needle and syringe.

Outside the house a man stood. "Are you the lady's husband?" I asked.

"No, that man you met on the trail going for his canoe to go fishing on the lake—that man is her husband," he replied.

Agitation overtook me. "What will he do if he loses his woman to a massive infection?"

"Well," he said, "no problem. He'll find another one." Stoic. Indifferent. And a lot worse.

NEVER CEASE TO WONDER

We were in the wood frame house as snug as could be. Around eight in the evening, the kids were about to go under their mosquito nets and into their hammocks. Someone was clapping at the gate. I went to see.

The men followed me in. One of them had fought with a wounded jaguar and was he a mess. "Escovado" could mean scrubbed clean, but in the irony of the river people, he was seen to be a real scoundrel.

That morning he had been scoring diagonal cuts in his trail of rubber trees to later make the circuit and collect the rubber milk. His buddy was nearby on another trail. As buddies they shared and shared alike.

Mr. Scoundrel saw a jaguar slip into a thicket of bamboo. He crept near it and saw the jaguar resting in this hideaway. Mr. Scoundrel should have whistled or somehow signaled for his buddy to go against this jaguar with him. Not ready to share the value of the hide of the jaguar, Mr. Scoundrel attempted a shot.

The shotgun was loaded with a heavy lead shot, but as he aimed, he was unaware that the shotgun barrel was impeded by a bamboo branch he did not see as he sighted along the barrel. BOOOOM! The wounded jaguar bounded out of the bamboo and slashed his back, his face, bit his arm, and did other injuries. His buddy heard the commotion and finished off the jaguar. It otherwise would have finished off Mr. Scoundrel.

It took most of the day by canoe to arrive at our house that evening. My tools of the trade were sterilized. I didn't know why, since this was going to be a mess. Others had put spider webs, manure and burned coffee grounds on the wounds to stop bleeding. What I did need was to borrow a spool of silk from Barbara' sewing kit. Our daughter Beth helped. One of our boys counted fifty-six lacerations that I had to sew.

Late that night we had done what was possible. The man knew we were believers. Mr. Scoundrel had relatives who also were followers of Jesus. So what did Mr. Scoundrel do when I helped him off our eating table? Not a word! No "thank you." Nothing. He walked out and was gone.

His first stop was to pray to his idol thanking this piece of plaster for saving his life. Mr. Scoundrel was too blind spiritually to see that the God of the universe had located one of his servants to be on the spot when his life would otherwise have ended with massive infection and festering wounds—all fifty-six of them.

King David had harsh words for idolaters:

Those who worship idols are disgraced--all who brag about their worthless gods--for every god must bow to him.

Psalm 97:7 (NLT)

Chapter 31: DOES IT MAKE A DIFFERENCE?

Does it really matter if people misread our motives for what we do? Why we do it? One could only wish that others could see life as we do, but it probably won't happen. Our role is to be and do regardless of whether we are misread or not.

I was out front of the house I had just built from boards sawed from trees felled in the jungle. I was quite proud, too, of my discovery of a varnish made from copaiba oils from that tree. Mixed half and half with gasoline, it went on all the new wood inside the house just like a high class varnish, which some later thought it was.

Between where I stood and the river was the dirt track that passed in front of our house. And there before my eyes was a large tug boat and a barge moored at the river's edge. In the shade of a nearby tree stood a tall, balding man puffing on a pipe, not what I had ever seen as being customary anywhere in the Amazon.

I surmised that he must be the tug boat captain. I walked over to introduce myself. "I am Alan Bachmann, and folks know me by my middle name which they can easily pronounce, so I am called "Pastor Luis." (I thought of some other names I wouldn't mention.) I expected this man to identify himself in some way, but he didn't. Oh well, I thought, that's the way some river men are.

The next day I was sent a note inviting me to appear at the "Nuns' Hospital." When I walked into the office, who is sitting behind the desk? No riverboat captain, as I first surmised the man with the pipe to be, but a man I would come to know as the most notable virologist in South America. I was soon to learn that a team called

"Project Rondon" had been instituted to introduce university students to the sociological conditions of the Brazilian population of the hinterlands. Marshal Rondon of some generations ago had strung telegraph cables across Indian tribal lands and thus was known as a pacifier of them.

The team had arrived unannounced as they were attempting to investigate the function or malfunction of various government-funded programs. One with the group was a Jewess of Interpol who used some seven languages. Some locals were caught with sticky fingers and a lot of dust was raised.

I was invited by Dr. Domingos to come into the office at the hospital where he sat. When we began to chat, I must say that at this moment I had no idea with whom I was talking.

"They tell me you do some doctoring to assist the population, but that you are not so credentialed in Brazil."

I imagined that Sister Klara had told him a story or two. "I trained in the USA only as a paramedic to care for my own family."

"How do you treat malaria?"

"Which of the three types of malaria do you mean?"

When he asked about Hansen's disease (leprosy), I spoke of the various forms it takes. We talked about the five main intestinal parasites, coetaneous leishmanaisis, tuberculosis, and such. I was just "talking shop." Dr. Domingos thanked me for my time and bid me good day.

I received a second invitation from him the following day. As I sat in front of his desk, he had a cheerful look on his face as he began to speak. "Alan, I know where you went to grade school, high school and all your further studies in Bible, linguistics, aviation, and training in the different hospitals in California. I represent Brazil's Minister of Health. I herewith give you a letter of commendation and gratitude for all you do for our people, and in so doing you charge not a cent. You may show this letter to anyone who may question your activities or your competency. You have our wholehearted support."

The Rondon Project team consisted of various elements among which were two finalists in medicine. I was called upon to "translate" the technical and totally correct use of university-level Portuguese to a simple language the river people could grasp. The Rondon Project folk could soon see that very few could follow their presentations to the population on public health, hygiene and nutrition. So there I was "translating."

AT LEAST HIS STORY SOUNDS GOOD

While the Rondon Project was in town, many university students from the big cities were actively involved with phases of the project. Those in the medical or dental field knew of my activities in this area. Competency was not in question. Those in this field were yet to apply their studies to the practical rigors of life.

One day the two medical students came to my house and asked me if I would take them to "see some of your many properties." I already knew that they thought, that the only reason this foreigner is here is to acquire large tracts of land for little or no money. I played dumb.

Off we went in my fast outboard, a Boston whaler with a fifty horsepower Mercury engine. Our first stop was at a port upriver called Paradise, which it surely wasn't. The manager of the plantation was well known. I introduced the two med students to Senhor Joaquim. He invited us to stay for a fish roast and quickly sent someone to the lake to bring back a large fish called a Tambaquí. With manioc meal and some fixings it is most delicious. We ate our fill. With much thanks to Joaquim, we departed.

The two med students said, "Now let's see some of your other plantations and lands." Off we sped to the rubber plantation and then a ranch of Sr. João Xixaro, father of Leonés. Late in the afternoon we returned to the port in front of our house. One of the two said, "Let the cat out of the bag."

In Brazil it is common to say, "Our house is your house" as a term of endearment and hospitality. I explained that I was received in the places we visited as if I were part of those who lived there. So when one of the med students said, "So all of these lands are yours? Do you have a title deed to all of this?"

I knew this was coming and replied with a smile. "All of the places we visited are owned by those we met. I go as a guest, and I am well received in most places. Hey, not even the house I built is mine. It belongs to the mission. The boat is mine only to serve others. It, too, is mission property."

They were quite disconcerted to have their bubble of suspicions burst. I enjoyed helping to educate them to a reality they had not yet experienced, but could take with them to enhance their understanding in the years to come.

They could believe me or not, but at least think, *At least his story sounds good.*

You are so sure of the way to God that you could point it out to a blind man. You think of yourselves as beacon lights, directing men who are lost in darkness to God.

Romans 2:19 TLB

Chapter 32: IT DOESN'T MATTER, BUT IT DOES HURT

What do you say and what do you do when others judge your motives by their value system even as perverse, or not, as that may be? They do judge by their values.

The mayor asked me to stop by his office. He held forth in a long room of a building dating before 1900. These offices are one level above the town square, with walkways, safe from rains and water. The furnishings were heavy, ornately carved wood chairs and a desk to match that suggested the antiquity of this place. I was invited to sit on a chair at the opposite end of this long room. Along both sides was an odd assortment of loafers, the mayor's lackeys, and a riverboat man or two. Some I had seen on board one boat or another.

Prefeitura na praça.

The drama opened with a frontal attack by the mayor. "I know you are digging gold and mining diamonds. Either you split 50/50 with me, or I'll bring in federal authorities to uncover your secrets."

This sounded like a good case of blackmail if I were doing as he evidently believed. I reflected on Abe Lincoln's remark that the best defense is no defense. "Your Excellency, "I replied, "you are the maximum authority in this municipality. If you so choose, please call in the authorities. I am at your service to present myself and my home as may be necessary." I went on to remind him, "I am always under the eye of the town's people and in their homes visiting the sick."

Well, the mayor blew up! He turned on me in a rage. Among other attacks, the most grave of offenses was to insult one's mother. This might incite a knifing or a shooting which is termed a "crime of passion" and is excusable as such. He tried that on me too. All I could do was pray that the Lord would keep my mouth shut, and I would not react. I could only be the person God made me to be as His Ambassador. Any other conduct would bring shame on God's name.

I was dumfounded to see that the mayor really believed what he was accusing me of doing. Some of his cronies whispered to me as if on my side against the mayor, that I should get up and "slam that guy."

I let the mayor run out of steam and did not pick up on any of his foul language or insults about my mother. Finally he calmed down. I rose very slowly, and as I did, I requested, "Excellency, permit me to leave and fulfill my responsibilities."

A nod gave me to understand I could go. As I walked across the room and came before him to go out the door, I said: "I am at your service for whatever help I can do."

He sneered at me. "I don't need you! I wouldn't even accept a cup of water from a poor person." As I looked across his desk, his drawer was open and a 38 revolver lay there ready to use.

I left the room, went down the stairs of this ancient wooden structure to come out on one side of the little town square. The bandstand stood in the middle. On the other side of the square was the bishop Dom Michael's church. I crossed the town square diagonally to the street that bordered the river. The river was to my left and the simple row of shops on my right. This little town was primitive, having no electricity, no phones, nothing.

I was drained emotionally. Should I stay on in this town with a jerk like that to contend with? About ten minutes along the river road I passed in front of the store of Dona Antonieta. As I passed, she stood at the door of her shop, greeted me, and asked me if I would like a Graviola popsicle (tropical fruit, which in fact was placed in a glass to be eaten with a spoon). I was so washed out all I could think of was clearing out of this town. I felt rejected, hurt, and misunderstood.

Culturally I could not refuse the gracious offer of a lady who sold this and many other products in her store. Why couldn't I refuse? Her offer was a gesture meant to gain the opportunity to say something. She was a highly respected widow whom many of the river people admired. My wife Barbara was in her sewing club.

Dona Antonieta sat at the little table with me. She could not have surprised me more when she said, "I know what the mayor just tried on you in his office." (I later learned that he had a hard rubber club and a pile of rock salt ready at the local jail to give me a going over if I had in any way reacted overtly).

When she told me she knew what the mayor had tried on me, I was sure she must have had a pair of ears in the mayor's room. While I was dragging my feet along the river road, that person got back to her and told her the story.

She looked at me with the eyes of a mother and full of compassion. "Dear Pastor, don't leave our town." (Did she know or guess what I was thinking?) "Look, we know you are a man of God. Please stay. This vile man will soon see his end and you will stay with our people." This dear lady was a practicing Roman Catholic, and she was speaking to my heart. I finished that graviola ice with a melted heart and a renewed purpose to stay on. Another ten minutes' walk up the river road and I was home to tell Barbara all that transpired.

What would the morning after bring? I heard a clap at the door. Someone was "calling" at our house. I opened the door surprised to see there stood the mayor who just the day before had declared, "I don't need you!"

"Billy the Kid" stood at the door wearing two matching pearl handled revolvers hanging from his hips in a fully loaded cartridge belt. "Pastor, I need you. Will you take me in your fast outboard to a rubber plantation?"

"I will, but you have to furnish the gasoline and oil for the trip." I agreed to bring my 50 hp Boston Whaler to the main river port and pick up the mayor there after I took on the gasoline and oil and mixed it.

This turned into quite a scenario. A few townspeople saw me or heard my boat pull into the port at the bottom of the stairs that disappeared into the river as it rose or fell with the season. When somebody saw the mayor's guy carrying the gas cans to my boat, the news travelled by "jungle vine" (word of mouth) with lightening speed. Here comes "Billy the Kid" with his pearl handled guns and sits himself in the bow, not taking his eyes off me. Away we went.

The comments made the rounds as I later learned. "Hey, this pastor slaps the mayor in the face without using his hand. Yesterday the mayor would have thought nothing of shooting the pastor and today it's the pastor who serves the mayor."

I looked at this experience in a different perspective. As an ambassador of the Lord, I am duty bound to represent Him who called me to be His ambassador.

As the story unfolded, the mayor, in his late forties, became very ill. Sister Klara at the hospital used a remedy all her own that caused the mayor to expel a tape worm that filled a liter bottle. I was called on to care for him for his extremely high blood pressure. In due course, he developed a renal malady. His kidneys were shutting down. A plane was called in to fly him to a hospital in the city where he succumbed.

It is exciting to walk into the unknown certainly aware that God knows and controls every situation that He places us in to be His Ambassador before those who do not know Him.

"The Lord is with me: I will not be afraid.
What can man do to me?"

King David, in Psalm 118.6 (KJV)

Port and stairs down to the river edge.

The cathedral on the right and a row of stores

Chapter 33: THE TREACHERY OF
COFFEE-MILK RIVER

The murky, muddy waters of the Madeira River swirled around
us for days as we journeyed, heading home from Manaus. If only the
taste were that of coffee and milk. Drink enough of it and you would
probably end up with sandbars in the loops of your intestines. On
board with me and my colleague was a very good boatman. Tando
asked for a ride home. Not one of us was any good at cooking, but that
would change as soon as we arrived home in another day of travel.

Our launch's little diesel engine growled like a Jaguar. Totally
rebuilt, the engine was carrying us up the Madeira River and home to
our waiting families. The Madeira River is 1,950 kilometers (about
1,300 miles) long in Brazil entering from Bolivia, flowing north to
where it joins the Amazon River. We made it safely by the huge
whirlpool near Borba then navigated the big rocks at "Conception." By
the next day we passed a safe distance from "Singing Rooster" below
Alligator Island. Three long days of the lower Madeira River lay
behind us since leaving Manaus, the hub city of Amazonas. We babied
the rebuilt engine, chugging along, running at a carefully reduced
RPM speed.

Late afternoon of day four, storm clouds blackened the sky. We
were coming up on Winner Island – (*Ilha do Vencedor*). The river was
at its lowest level of the year, thirty five to forty feet down from its
high water mark. There was only one channel by the island which ran
along its western side. I nosed the launch into this dangerous passage
between the rocks that showed us their teeth. Strong currents funneled

between these rocks. The river offered no options to avoid facing the onslaught of this powerful coffee-colored flow.

My time on the river had taught me much. Above all, experience gave me great respect for this monster that had devoured many a riverboat. The Madeira was one of the most treacherous of rivers in the Amazon system, and the many dangers along its length presented plenty of threats.

Lightening tore open the black clouds. The din of the motor did not soften the thunder's roar. At the controls, I observed that we were not gaining against the current in our passage through the rocks. Looking to the right, the current was cutting along a very high, straight-upriver bluff. I accelerated the diesel engine just a bit, hoping to gain headway against the current between the rocks.

A moment later, when it seemed we would make it through, I heard a sickening *clunk*. The engine froze and died. I spun the wheel to the right. No rocks in the way. The current carried us against this sheer river bluff, higher than the mast on our launch.

As we bumped against it, our helper on board cut footholds with a machete and nimbly climbed to the top. We tossed him a long length of chain secured to the bow of the launch. While he held the launch against the river bluff, we climbed up these footholds he had cut. Our eyes froze for an instant on a crack that was opening along the bluff. We were more than alarmed.

Taking a turn on one tree stump and then another, we quickly let the current ease the launch along. In a bit, the bluff slanted down to an eddy in the current. Here we could secure the launch. We stood trembling with exhaustion, knee deep in the river.

Suddenly a very loud "whoosh" reached our ears. A huge wave surged across the river. That crack where we had climbed to the top of the bluff dumped tons of earth from the edge of that high bluff into the river. The current had undercut that bluff on which we had been standing moments earlier.

In all of this an inexplicable peace came upon us. When you knew the one who is Master of creation; the river, the storms, the wind and the fury, yes, the calm that settled over this ferocious land, there was no other place for His Ambassador to be than where God had placed him.

A river trader I knew came chugging up this same channel. As his boat bit into the onslaught of the current, he slowed up and pulled in just behind the eddy of current where we were with our broken-down engine. Sr. Lourival offered to tow us home. He secured his boat's gang plank across the bow and tied us out alongside. Such an arrangement was safer than towing behind his big launch. The expected arrival home was now three days away instead of one. Our benefactor was a river trader, so he stopped in ports here and there. My colleague was new to the Amazon, and did he suffer! He seemed to pace back and forth on the deck as if this would speed us on our way.

Travel on the mighty Madeira never became easier, but it was part of my "Ambassadorial" duties. I probably represented my Lord and King more in the adversities of river life than when things seemed to go along so smoothly. Even when there was no moment for a spoken message, character spoke loudly 24/7 (for good or for bad). The letter God had written in our hearts was indelible and readable by all who cared to open their eyes to see what He wanted us to show to others.

"You show that you are a letter from Christ, written not with ink but with the Spirit of the living God on tablets of human hearts."

Apostle Paul to the Church in Corinth, Greece.
2 Corinthians 3:3 (NIV)

Chapter 34: THE GOD WHO IS THERE

Written by Barbara

Alan and I lived seven days' travel by boat from Manaus, upriver in the small village of Humaitá. We started the ministry when only 800 people lived there. This story's moment took place at home while Alan was one day upriver, camped in the jungle, with a youth retreat. Yes, with hammocks, mosquito nets, the teens with Alan lived off the river and the jungle.

At home with our kids, I felt bad and went from bad to worse. In a few hours, I was completely debilitated with a kidney problem. Two steps were taken. I sent a boat upriver in search of Alan, and I sent a neighbor to the hospital. The very elderly German nun, dear Sister Klara, whom my husband helped many times in the hospital, came to our home on foot, through the mud, to administer an intravenous solution. She came to give me a succession of intravenous feedings every few hours, each time more than a half mile through the mud.

The boatman sent upriver found Alan and handed him the note I had scribbled in my trembling hand, "Come quickly. I'm very sick."

When the boatman gave him the note, Alan knew something was really wrong. No greeting. No small talk. And then looking down he handed Alan the note. A young man with Alan on this jungle retreat perceived the situation to be unusual. "Pastor, go. I'll take care of your hammock and things."

When Alan arrived, the boatman pulled in at the river bank and let him off right in front of our house at the river's edge. He climbed the embankment of the river. Approaching the wooden gate to enter our yard, the women of the congregation sat in a group. Alan was afraid to greet them, not knowing if I was still alive. For this reason he hesitated to open the gate. If the women, who had just finished praying, did not greet him, it would be because I had passed away. If they greeted him, then he knew I was still alive. They greeted Alan.

"I was so relieved to see Barbara, but she looked terrible," Alan later said. "I've seen too many sick people, and all sorts of scenes went through my mind."

After spending a few moments with me, he trudged through the mud in search of some answer or resource. What, if any, recourse was there to alleviate my situation? Down river with the current, it would take some five days by riverboat to the city of Manaus.

Passing one of the merchants' stores, Senhor Antonio asked Alan, "How's your wife?" The whole village knew Sister Klara was giving me intravenous feedings. "I don't think she'll survive, Senhor," Alan replied, "even five days by riverboat with the current in a hammock."

"There's a twin engine plane that belongs to the company who is going to build the Trans Amazon Highway through here," Sr. Antonio told Alan. "They cut a dirt airstrip with a bulldozer about two kilometers outside the town."

Senhor Antonio offered the only pickup in the village and ordered his nephew to take Alan out to talk with the pilot of the airplane. He asked for passage for me to go to Manaus, where the plane was headed. The pilot said the plane was fully loaded, and company regulations did not allow carrying non-company personnel.

Alan thanked the pilot, and the nephew of Sr. Antonio returned Alan to inform Senhor Antonio of the pilot's refusal to take me to Manaus.

Sad and discouraged, Alan slogged the kilometer through the mud back to our house to tell me the sad news. Hardly had he arrived when we heard the pickup slipping and sliding in the mud, and honking as it stopped in front of our house. When Alan looked out, of all people, he saw Senhor Antonio, grinning from ear to ear. Alan did not understand why.

Then Sr. Antonio shouted, "Stuff some things in a suitcase. Your wife is going on the plane to Manaus."

In a few moments, Alan carried me to Antonio's waiting pickup with a few clothes he quickly put in a little suitcase. Antonio drove me right to the aircraft, all ready to take off as soon as I was on board and strapped in my seat. No other passengers were on this plane. In flight, the pilot contacted the tower at Manaus to inform our family doctor, Dr. Wallace Ramos de Oliveira, who met the plane to receive me. His diagnosis ruled out the worst and treated my condition. The rest is history.

God did the impossible, as we later learned this story.

When Alan told Antonio of the pilot's refusal, Senhor Antonio went back and told the pilot, "Your road company will build this stretch of the Trans-Amazon Highway (Highway? It was dirt all the way.) and I am the Federal Tax Collector. I think we should understand each other. I sent our friend, Pastor Alan, who asked you to please take his wife to Manaus, as she is between life and death. You refused to take this man's wife?"

"But he's a Protestant," the pilot said.

"He's our friend, He's my friend. He treats all the sick in our village and works with the nuns in their hospital. On my behalf I ask you to take his wife to Manaus in your plane."

Senhor Antonio had intervened on our behalf. I arrived safe and sound in Manaus. Because of the over-ruling providence of our gracious God in the affairs of men, God is never frustrated to accomplish His will.

Barbara back home in Humaitá as healthy as ever.

"O Lord God of Israel, there is no God like you in all of heaven and earth. You are the God who keeps his kind promises to all those who obey you and who are anxious to do your will.

2 Chronicles 6:14

Chapter 35: IN THE RIVER

The steamy heat of a tropical night pressed upon us. We were sitting in a screened-in area. Jungle sounds, so much a part of everything, can go unnoticed. They change through the night almost becoming a clock if you listen for them. It was relaxing here by the river. As we talked my mind went back in time.

Where we sat talking had not so long a time back been dense jungle. On the outskirts of Porto Velho, on the edge of the great Madeira River, we were on the premises of a linguistic group. These folk are dedicated to reducing spoken tribal languages to a written form using internationally defined symbols for any sound the vocal system can produce.

I recalled a vacation from our river town of Humaitá when I came here to Porto Velho (Old Port) and was asked to help survey some jungle for the linguistic base as it was then envisioned. How could I help? I ended up carrying a surveyor's tripod through swamp and jungle to lay out this huge tract of land where simple wood frame thatch houses now stood.

The land survey was a gooey go of it. All kinds of leaches and bugs to latched onto my body surface for a ride until I got out of the swamp where I could deal with these invaders.

I had been in swamps many times. Back where we lived, we had cut the logs from the swamps and floated them out to hand saw into boards when we built our house. If one were a smoker, the tobacco in the blood stream would cause these guys to drop off, not being able to cope with the nicotine. I learned this from my doctor grandfather who used leeches to convince smokers to drop the habit, long before science knew the ills of smoking.

Our reminiscing and revelry was broken by the sound of a river ship blasting its horn. The two missionaries remembered that they were waiting for a shipment of aviation gas for their amphibian plane. The ship would hold off against the current just on the edge of the channel of the Madeira River now in full flood season. But where was the boat or canoe to go get the barrels of aviation gas as they would pitch them off the deck? Deck cargo was the "gravy" of the ship captain. The fuel had been paid for before shipping.

No canoe or boat was there, so now what? I was more at home in and around the water and always had swim trunks (with very tight legs) so in the water I went with a coil of line (some call it rope) being fed out as I swam toward the ship. When those on board saw me in the flood lights of the deck, they began pitching the aviation gasoline barrels into the river. There were eight or so barrels. I swam the barrels into a cluster and got a line around some of them. The rest I "swam" by pushing the other barrels farther into the eddy of the current where they would not get away from me.

All of a sudden a chill went through me. Underneath these waters lurked giant catfish of some grotesque descriptions. A man had been swallowed by one, but that's a story for another time. What was I doing out here being bait for these denizens of the deep?

The result was that I was giving the same help to our linguistic friends, in this case the pilots, to do what they were not so apt to do. Maybe the ship was not expected until the next day. Obviously I did not end up as food for the fish.

This same town of Porto Velho is today a booming city at the headwaters of the Madeira River where it comes over a mix of eighteen waterfalls and dangerous rapids from Bolivia where three rivers – the Beni, Madre de Dios and Riberalta feed their waters into this one "River of Wood." Thirty days up one of these is a fort built in the 1700's with a tunnel under the river from Brazil to Bolivia. I had been to "Fort Prince." I had seen its dungeon and signs of some of the mysteries surrounding this place.

More than two centuries ago, an attempt was made to build a canal around these waterfalls and cataracts. It failed. Then later and finally, a railroad was built around these 200 kilometers of treacherous river.

The story is told in a book in Portuguese (A Ferrovia do Diabo). "The Devil's Railroad" asserts that each cross-tie cost one life to malaria, other tropical diseases or to slaughter by Indians. Men from many nations came to find work on the Devil's railroad. Some remained in the Candelabra Cemetery. Others stayed on in the community or moved somewhere else in Brazil.

Transatlantic freighters came up the Madeira River bringing equipment, material and supplies to the river port at the lower end of the falls. Some ships foundered, sinking after being battered by winds and waves of tropical tempests. Others sank after striking rocks along the way. The arriving ships made an effort to try one location too close to the falls and then settled back to a former location, thus the name "Old Port."

Porto Velho today is a boom town. Farmers ship tons of soy beans downriver. The airport once near to everything has moved far out of town. Hydro electric flow-through turbines have been installed so there is no typical barrier to hold back silt-laden waters. The electric power it generates makes it the second largest generator in Brazil. The population is exploding. Building is going on everywhere – schools, hospitals, supermarkets all pop up like mushrooms.

Our son-in-law Pastor Jonas and daughter Beth develop church start-ups. The presence of the gospel message is imperative to bring God's peace in a world of chaos. Our son Judson went from here to become an airline captain of international passenger jets. Daughters Karis, a dental surgeon, and Katrina, a medical doctor, serve in this region.

When I waded through jungle to survey, or swam the river that night, who could dream what all this would become some day, down the road of life?

...for the LORD will be at your side and will keep your foot from being snared.

King Solomon, in Proverbs 3:26 (NIV)

Chapter 36: MORE HOT WATER

A reputation follows one in these remote regions of the Amazon. It fits the saying, "You can run but you can't hide." They'll find you.

The riverboat I was on was one of many that carry passengers and freight up and down the 1,950 kilometers of the Madeira River. I was on my way upriver toward home in Porto Velho, where we would arrive in about three days. We were tied up at a floating dock in the town of Nova Olinda on the lower end of the Madeira. I relaxed in my hammock as freight was off loaded.

Leaving passengers unstrung their hammocks to disembark. Others, coming on board, hung theirs. The deck could get quite full, and one lived in close proximity to the hammocks on either side. Some were slung lower and some higher, always trying to squeeze one more in place. At least while in port, the idling diesel engine gave out less noise, and I could almost carry on a conversation without shouting.

"Yes, he's on board, " I heard from down on the dock. Who, I wondered.

The engine shut down. Silence.

A moment later the riverboat Captain came to my hammock on the upper deck. "Doctor, there is an extreme emergency in the village. Please, go talk to the brother of this woman."

Intrigue? What was going on? That fact that the engine had been shut down was unusual. The captain was typically in a hurry to be on his way. Time was money.

I climbed out of my hammock and went down the stairs to the lower deck of this giant wooden structure. On the dock I met the brother of a woman who was in the maternity area of what was called a hospital. These hospitals, loosely called, were sometimes in the hands of political cronies or, at best, people not prepared for the responsibility. They had tried to deliver the woman's child and had been very unsuccessful. To go into this environment and intervene was not to my liking. I would get all the blame and no help. However, I said nothing and waited and listened.

The woman's brother saw one solution. Get his sister to Manaus, the hub city of the Amazon. He asked me if I would accompany his sister. He had a fast river launch that could make the trip in less than eighteen hours. I saw that my upriver travel home was going to be delayed. Barbara never worried. When I would get home from such diversions, she was always waiting patiently.

I consented to go. Shortly the lady was put onboard her brother's launch. I got my hammock and luggage from the passenger boat, no longer heading upriver and home. This woman was in dire straights. Her labor had become inactive. She was probably close to exhaustion. There was hope we could make it downriver to Manaus and to the government's Balbina Maternity Hospital. I never did get in my hammock, but stayed by the woman just to observe how she was doing in her hammock. There, at least she would be free of the vibrations and rest as well as possible.

Arriving at a port in one of the waterways that surround the city, I found a pay phone and called my friend, Dr. Wallace, who had delivered our kids and was Barbara's OB-GYN doctor. I described the situation of the lady. "Get her to Balbina Maternity, "he said very decisively. "I'll meet you there." I found a cab and pleaded with the cab to take us very gently to Balbina.

We got there but Dr. Wallace hadn't arrived. I hoped he would be along any moment. The receptionist, granddaughter of Japanese immigrants, knew me from somewhere. I explained the drama. She replied that the Director of Balbina was out "for a minute" (that was a phrase that could mean anything from minutes to hours), "but you can get the lady to the delivery room."

There I met two of the most hardened, calloused midwives I have ever seen. Both were functionaries of the state. Was I ever desperate. To come this far and then fall into the hands of these two?

I took over, hoping that any minute I would see our Doctor Wallace appear. We placed the woman on the table. Those two stood there. "Prep the woman for delivery. Bladder and intestines emptied. Get a tray of instruments for any eventuality. And medications stat!" I named the ones she needed.

These two had no idea who I was, and I came on heavy to get some action. She was prepped. Bladder and intestines had been cleared so now, with no impediments, the baby started its descent. The midwives "caught" the baby and did not seem even to clear the airway, so I did and clamped off the umbilical cord. I was very upset, but kept my mouth shut.

Then before the placenta came, she started hemorrhaging. One of the two midwives said so in a loud voice the mother could hear, "I don't think she will escape this hemorrhaging." Dopes!

I climbed on a stool and put my fist in the tummy over the inferior vena cava artery and at the same time gave orders for medication – "STAT" intravenous and intra muscular.

Those two midwives jumped around, more afraid of me than they were concerned with the mother. The baby was doing well, thank the Lord. We got things under control, and once the placenta was out, the situation took a real turn for the better. Bleeding stopped.

About this time, the Director of Balbina Maternity Hospital walked by the delivery room and saw me through the glass that surrounded the upper half. She walked on.

A moment later, the receptionist came to the door. "The Director asked who this new doctor is, and was he listed to work in the maternity hospital?"

"Tell her you have asked the question, and I will be free of this delivery in a moment," I replied.

Seeing that the mother and baby were now okay, I washed up and was gone. The two midwives had never asked my name and told the Director how the case had been handled. Because there were no repercussions and everything turned out well, the Director of Balbina dropped her interest in the matter. It was a feather in her bonnet.

Doctor Wallace never did show up, and never said a word about the matter. Maybe he knew more than I imagined or had more hope in my action than I could know.

I stayed in the mission apartment in Manaus until I could arrange passage on a riverboat back up the Madeira. The door was open with just the screen door present to let any available breath of air circulate. I heard clapping and went to the door. It was the brother of the woman I had delivered at the maternity hospital. He had the biggest smile.

"How is your sister doing?" I asked. "And how's the baby?"

He was so excited to tell me his sister and the baby were both well, beyond his wildest dream.

He pulled out a roll of bills that would choke a horse. "How can I thank you for saving the life of my sister and her baby? I want to pay you."

"I can't accept payment from poor or well-off. As a servant of God, I was only doing what I could in His Name. Besides, I'm not a credentialed Physician." I was talking to one of the wealthiest merchants on the Madeira River.

"Isn't there some way, then, that I can help with your mission in life?"

"Well, the little church in Manicore is hoping to acquire a little portable pump organ."

Where there was nonexistent or very poor electrical current, the portable pump organ played well as long as the organist's feet kept pumping. And it can be carried about. Electric keyboards were not yet invented.

He gave me a pile of money and told me to go buy the organ. "I'm pleased to do some little thing to help."

The real story may only unfold in eternity. Here was a man who saw in us a value system of compassion at any and all risks to serve God and serve others. Would this man see the real story behind the story?

Jesus said,

"Let your light shine before others, that they may see your good deeds and glorify your Father in heaven."

Matthew 5:16 (NIV)

Chapter 37: THE POWERS OF DARKNESS

The machinations of Darkness snare multitudes in its art to capture their minds and hearts.

I was on board a riverboat, comfortably swinging in my hammock with the boat's motion as we plied the Madeira River. I had been reading my Bible, which I kept in a leather zipper cover. It lay on my chest as I snoozed. Someone shook my hammock to awake me.

"I'll read your hand," said a woman.

Searching my mind for a reply, I asked her: "What did you say?"

She repeated the offer to "read my hand." In this context, the offer implied that she would tell me my future by reading the palm of my hand.

I looked at her with a smile. "Oh, you're too late! I have a book that tells me all about my past, how to live in the present, and it even tells me of my future destiny."

The lady was so excited. "Sell me the book!"

I told her it was mine and I couldn't sell it, but I knew a store where she could buy one in Manaus.

"What is the name of the book?

When I told her it was the "Bíblia Sagrada," she made an exclamation and the sign of the cross as people do to avoid an "evil eye" or "bad luck," and she was gone.

In the earlier chapter, "A Man Called Julian," I told of how Pastor Julian had warned "the Colonel," owner of a rubber plantation, that he dare not blaspheme God. Later, searchers found the Colonel in the jungle dead as a stone. The powers of darkness rule in the lives of many.

THE DOMAIN OF THE POWER OF DARKNESS

I accepted the invitation of a merchant, Aurelio, to treat the people in his region. Many were his customers. His house was situated on a point of land between the Madiera and the outpouring of the huge Acará Lake, which a century or more in the past may have been a channel of the Madeira River. I stayed in his home that night to get an early start on the day.

During the evening meal, I learned a bit about the history of this family. The father, deceased, had been a Spiritualist. When he passed away, Aurelio wrote to the ones who sent him the Journal on Spiritualism from Portugal to inform that his father had passed away. This man told me that he wrote even though the Journal had stopped arriving the month of his father's death, which had left Portugal three months before. It took three months to arrive from Portugal to their place on the river. The Spiritualists in Portugal wrote thanking the son and informed him, "We knew here from our 'sources' the very day your father passed on."

Looking around the room while we ate, I noticed what appeared to be a shallow crib. Actually, this was their "house of saints." They worshipped these images and attributed power to them. Was this an improvement on Spiritualism?

The following morning there were so many people to care for, as Aurelio had done too good a job of informing people of my coming. I sensed a strange atmosphere. Folks were quiet and seemed in some way fearful. I soon learned that the local priest had created a climate of fear. He had told them, "This man is from the pit of hell. Treat him like a fox in the hen house. A clubbing will make short work of him."

Before long, the manner in which I showed compassion and treated each patient allowed me to move along attending to each person in need.

Down the road of life two things surfaced. Aurelio showed up in Humaitá after he had converted to Christ and studied enough to become a lay evangelist.

The years rolled along. On a visit I made to a church in Porto Velho, a woman came to me with her grown son and a big smile. "Back at the Acará, when he was a boy and because of what the priest told everybody, he was scared to death of you. By your patience and love you won his confidence. We learned about Jesus and now we are all believers in Him."

Their gods are merely man-made things of silver and of gold. They can't talk or see, despite their eyes and mouths! Nor can they hear, nor smell, nor use their hands or feet, nor speak! And those who make and worship them are just as foolish as their idols are.

Psalm 115:4-8 (TLB)

Madeira River has more islands than one can imagine. On the island of Tambaquí (also the name of a fish), three men were trekking to their fields to burn piles of branches and brush from land they had cleared away to make ready for planting. This was at the height of the dry season, when rains are sparse.

Hoes over the shoulders and machetes in hand, just arriving to burn, it began to rain. One of the three men began to curse God for bringing rain. His language was vile. The two with him warned him that maybe this God of heaven was not like the gods we make. Maybe this God was listening.

These people were so accustomed to worshipping idols made with their hands, they could not easily conceive of the all-knowing, ever-present God of heaven. The two friends' warnings went unheeded. After all, this guy thought he was special. He was an idol maker and was paid well to repair and paint idols that termites and time had damaged.

In the middle of one of his ravings, all of a sudden his mouth went crooked. The rest of his body was not affected (different from a cerebral vascular accident). As I was told, not even his closest friends or wife could understand a thing he mumbled. None are so blind as those who create the gods of their imagination. In Psalm 115, the first eight verses describe this blindness. "They become like them, those who make them and those who worship them."

STAY, BUT DO NOT SPEAK IN HIS NAME

A stretch of the Madeira is called the Coast of the Jaguar. The sand bar that comes out of the river in the dry season is Jaguar Beach. Along here is a huge plantation known as Jacob's Cut, a name given because in high water a small boat can go through this cut and reduce river travel by hours. The path cuts through the jungle around back of the plantation.

The main building was a very spacious house. The biggest room consisted of board benches and a big table. Idols surrounded it along the walls. This scenario was nothing new to me and didn't impede my attention to the sick.

A very old and sinister man lived in this region. He might show up mysteriously anywhere at any moment.

I had just tied up the launch, easily done. The river was in full flood, so I just walked off the gang plank with a shoulder loaded with baggage. The biggest, on the bottom, my case of medicines, the next one, slightly smaller, held my instruments, a cookie sheet, an alcohol squirt bottle, cotton, etc. On top sat a wind-up Victrola and a few 78 RPM records with sung hymns.

I carried this paraphernalia right to the table. I was about to unpack when the old, sinister man appeared. He sneered at me. "You can treat the sick and extract teeth, but I forbid you to speak His name."(I had not yet even declared in whose Name I had come).

In a moment, God gave me a reply for this evil man of the darkness. "If I cannot serve in His name, he taught His followers to stamp the mud from their feet and depart." The people waiting showed real fear of this evil one. They were sure he could cast a spell of punishment on them. I picked up my boxes, put them back on my shoulder, and was soon on board and away downriver.

Some months later, João, the fellow I had been with when we visited with "Jake the Cripple," was travelling to this same Coast of the Jaguar. João, with his wife and two kids, had been travelling from the high region of the Marmelos River in his palm-covered little diesel boat.

João had set out at dusk to arrive by morning on the Madeira above the Coast of the Jaguar. He was going to preach and help the sick. I had taught him the rudiments of diagnosing, worms, anemia, malaria (in one of the three types) and he could spot Hansen's disease (leprosy) and had learned how to give anesthetic and extract teeth.

On his run down the Marmelos River, several incidents marked the journey. With a waving *lamparina*, someone on shore called him into their river port, full of stumps and debris. The man thought João was a river trader.

João was very upset as it put his launch and propeller in danger. Further along, his little girl got out of her hammock, picked up his Bible and ripped a page from it. He spanked her and was very angry. Before leaving this peaceful river, the fuel injector on the cylinder of the diesel plugged up. The engine stopped. João took a thin wire from his guitar and finally unplugged the injector, got the engine running, restrung the wire, and tuned his guitar.

When he arrived shortly after dawn, he left his wife and kids onboard asleep. He went up to the location to see who might already be waiting. And who showed up? It was that vicious old man that everybody feared.

He directed himself to João. "And you're going to tell people how to follow your Jesus? A fine one you are! You got mad at the man who signaled you into his port. You spanked your daughter because she ripped a page from your Bible. Your injector blocked fuel flow, and you had to use a wire from your guitar. And you are going to speak to these people about Jesus?"

João recognized that humanly speaking, no one could know of these three happenings. He looked at the man. "Who are you?"

With an evil smirk the man said: "I was along to tempt you." He let out a sinister laugh.

"In the name of Jesus and by the power of His blood, I order you to depart," said João. The man was gone in a flash.

João had a full day of serving the people. The story of João repudiating the man by the authority of our Lord travelled far and wide on the "Jungle Vine."

From the time of my experience with this man at the plantation at "Jacobs Cut" a few years passed, and I had set up a clinic downriver in Manicoré. One day a woman and her daughter came to the clinic. I had no idea from where they had come, and it didn't matter. She had a tumor on her back, which I removed surgically as she could no longer carry a basket of manioc root from her plantings. I also did surgery on her daughter with a cleft lip, too much to tell here. But they were from Jacob's Cut as I write about later on.

YOU HARVEST WHAT YOU PLANT

Finishing touches of the trowel on the red-colored cement floor brought a sigh of relief. The deacon and I were looking forward to this place receiving many to hear of the one true God and His Son Jesus.

Orlando worked with us. He was good with a light touch on the trowel and a paid helper who had a job with the civilian branch of the Brazilian Air Force, beginning to build an air strip outside the village. The three of us worked together on the cement floor. The little church looked out over the mighty Madeira River. We would soon inaugurate it. The Amazon heat and humidity had drained our energies, but we were done.

The deacon and I talked, expressing our hope that God would make Himself known to these people through the Biblical point of view of man. The little church would be a point of encounter for many to hear the message of forgiveness of sin and eternal life.

A cloud of gloom came over Orlando as he listened. We watched. He seemed very emotionally upset. What was Orlando up to? He went up to the pulpit and began to mock God in a most foul manner. At first we thought he was making fun of us. The stark reality that Orlando was dead serious shocked us both. Like most in this community, Orlando worshipped idols, images that represent saints and beings that really do not exist.

Demons used idol worship to control people. It was one of the practices that God most condemned from early Old Testament writings. The village was fraught with open immorality. If the people could cover their god with a sheet so he couldn't see, "anything goes."

We pleaded with Orlando to stop speaking so viciously against God. "Orlando, God hears you and will not let these attacks on His name go without punishment. Please stop now."

He derided us, and it seemed that we could only remove him physically. Suddenly, he stopped and walked out of the new church building as if in a trance.

The incident unfolded the next day as later told by his wife and witnesses to the drama.

The next morning Orlando was due at work at the air strip, which meant that he would pedal out on his bicycle to get there. At the time he worked on a crew building a gravel air strip for our village of 1,200.

That morning his wife called him to get out of bed, leave the comfort of the straw mattress, and get on with it.

He gestured to his wife to come to his bedside. She came and chided him for not arising. In a weak voice he asked her for a kiss. Having done so, Orlando waved to her as if to say "goodbye." She was upset and somewhat confused. He didn't get out of bed.

Later that morning, a Brazilian Air Force plane landed out at the air strip that was being built. A military doctor was on board. Learning of the mysterious behavior of Orlando from one of their civilian workers, the doctor was entreated to go see Orlando. A jeep drove the doctor over the trail to Orlando's house to examine him.

The doctor rose from the bedside and spoke to Orlando's wife in the kitchen. "My dear lady, there is no point in taking Orlando on the plane to a hospital several flight hours away. I can find no physical ailment, yet I believe your husband will be dead by noon."

He was.

We had tried to tell Orlando that he should not deceive himself into thinking he was talking to one of his idols. We told Orlando that God will not be mocked. Whatever a man produces, he will collect on it. He will receive retribution in kind. If Orlando thought we were speaking from our own head, he was soon to know that we spoke in God's name.

This sad conclusion to a man's life became quite well known.

The apostle Paul said it clearly in speaking to some difficult people of Galatia.

"God is not mocked. As a man plants,
so shall he also harvest."

Galatians 6:7

SET FREE

I was standing on a street corner in Manus, normally a very busy one near the Amazon Opera House. However, being a holiday, even the magazine stand was closed. It was one which promoted Spiritism.

I observed a fellow nearby who looked rather unsettled. He looked over at me. I smiled. "Why is the magazine stand closed?" he asked me.

It seemed to be more a question of frustration. "Is there something in particular you are looking for?"

"I came from up north near the Venezuelan border. I've seen some powerful works of enchantment that put people into trances. I'm in search of this power so I can control people."

I told him that I knew of a book, actually a collection of sixty-six books, all written under the guidance of one author. The writer, over the centuries, had shown himself to be all powerful and all knowing.

"Where can I buy this book?"

I pointed up the street that goes behind the Military Secondary School. An evangelical book shop was located across the street. "If you can go by there tomorrow to the bookstore, I'll show you the book." At the time I didn't mention that this powerful book floats on water! That's how we get it to people in the jungle.

He did. I sold him a Bible. Weeks later he appeared again. He had closed himself away for weeks and read the Bible from cover to cover. He was vibrant, joyful, and very firm to know that through Jesus, the Son of God, he now had access and direct communion with God. Out of darkness into light!

Jesus made it crystal clear when He said,
"I am the light of the world. Whoever follows me will never walk in darkness, but will have the light of life."

John 8:12 (NIV)

Jesus said,
"I am the resurrection and the life. Anyone who believes in me will live, even after dying."

John 11:25 (NLT)

Chapter 38: THE CLINIC

We had moved back to the village of Manicoré, where we began our life in the Amazon. Much had changed, and much was the same.

When we first lived there, electrification was just becoming available, but only for an hour or so in the evening. The lights would come on – one small light bulb per house. Just before they turned the diesel generator off, they would dim the already dim lights three times, warning us to quickly light a candle or an Aladdin lamp.

There had been a walkway on either side of a "street" filled with high grass where pigs ran loose and wallowed in the mud in all of this. One mayor had decreed that everyone pen up their pigs. Everyone penned their pigs, and then we were overrun by snakes. A pig has such a layer of fat that by the time the snake's venom reached the blood stream, it was so dissipated that it had virtually no effect on the pigs. Also, a pig has a better nose than a dog, and they would detect the snakes and kill and eat them. The mayor "back tracked" on his edict, and the pigs again kept us pretty free of snakes.

Now that we were living in this village again, the electricity was being generated by steam turbines fired by volumes of wood from the jungle. We now had lights in our homes through most of the evening, and there was also some lighting on the streets.

The clinic I created consisted of a waiting area with wooden benches in our front yard, which often spilled over into our living room, a reception area with simple chairs. Adjacent to this waiting room was my clinic office with a window to the front of the house. The "windows" were built by my colleague and were simple horizontal boards that could be set at any angle depending on the weather. They either let in the sun or kept out the rain, and also allowed for ventilation. My clinic office held a desk, a chair, and a very old dental chair. The patients usually sat in the dental chair while I asked them how they felt and did an examination. Next to the dental chair was a glass case with all of my instruments and other paraphernalia so that they were easily accessible. A table on the other side of the room held a small sterilizer for my instruments, a microscope, centrifuge, glass slides, and stains.

What I liked to call my "secret weapon" was the fact that the rooms had walls only as high as where the roof tile met the side of the house. The rooms had no ceilings, so the voices from the visitor's room were easily overheard in the adjacent room where I was taking care of a patient. This structural feature allowed me to hear what they were telling each other and might forget when talking to the "doctor." I was blessed with the gift of being able to listen to at least two conversations and hold a conversation with another person simultaneously.

Our morning breakfast routine consisted of eating banana porridge and bread with coffee. Our kids went after the bread at dawn from our baker's wood-fired oven. We brewed good, strong, locally-roasted coffee heavily dosed with reconstituted powdered milk.

By 7 a.m. our yard was filled with many people from the village, nearby lakes, and the river. Some had come from great distances, but they knew they would not be sent away and told to come back another day. Our daughter Beth had a stack of numbered squares of cardboard to hand out to those waiting for medical care. Using a "first come, first served" basis could have relegated mothers with new babies and the very frail and elderly to a long wait. As Beth greeted each person, she could tell without asking which lake or river they were from by the greeting or accent. New mothers and the elderly were given the lowest numbers, ensuring that they received preferential treatment time-wise.

As each person came into my office, I usually took their blood pressure and looked in the backs of their eyes with the ophthalmoscope. Certain types of hypertension could be detected, as well as indications of some anomalies. Their ears were also checked. I quite often discovered that in someone" hard of hearing," their deafness was caused by an excess of wax or dried-up wax.

A typical day in my life in this town followed a simple pattern. As a rule I didn't stop for lunch until everyone had been seen and sent on their way. Approximately twenty to thirty people came to the clinic each day, usually not more than forty. After my mid-day meal, I might visit someone too sick to come to the clinic. This was not an everyday occurrence, but it might even mean making some late night visits.

In the evening I taught at the local high school. The challenge was to prepare future teachers for the early years of grammar school. The Municipal Director of Education asked me to teach some general science to a group of people designated to become primary teachers.

After I arrived home from teaching around ten each evening, my task was to use the microscope and process that day's collection of specimens. The patients who had left these would come by in the morning for the results and probably a prescription. The microscope helped to verify the presence of more than one type of intestinal parasite, malaria, or anemia.

There were times when this routine was interrupted as I turned into a "delivery boy," which was fun and yet hard work to assist a mother in giving birth. There was probably no greater thrill for me on the human level than to help bring a new life into the world. In another dimension, the greatest satisfaction was to see God at work in a life to transform that person from spiritual darkness to the light of His Son Jesus.

As the medical needs of the people diversified, I began to schedule one day just for teeth and/or elective surgery. Even the young people wanted teeth extracted, but instead I wanted to restore their teeth. I had a simple little electric bench drill which did the job. When they saw that teeth could be filled, it gave them hope that their teeth could be saved. They no longer had to live with the old mentality of "if it hurts, pull it." I also had to schedule "elective intervention" for those who came for a consultation that needed some work performed with a scalpel.

For me, it was a chance to be creative, I enjoyed repairing cleft lips on the young. Performing surgeries to remove tumors or reconstructing a shot-up hand or broken arm came with the territory. Of course, some of these surgeries could not be scheduled and were handled as they occurred.

During one of my travels along the river I visited a very large rubber plantation with the goal of helping the people and showing them what Jesus had done with my life. After securing the launch, I carried my paraphernalia to the main building and placed it on a central table. A grizzly old man came up to me.

"What are you going to do here?"

I thought that seemed pretty obvious. "I am here to treat the sick in the name of the One who sent me."

This grizzly old man was the head of the spirit worshippers. He was from the pit of Hell. He told me all about myself and defied me to speak the name of the One who sent me. I hadn't yet said the name of Jesus, but he knew!

"You can stay if you don't mention His name."

"If I can't speak of the One who sent me?"

He told me to stomp the mud from my feet and leave that place. This was the same thing Jesus told his disciples, in Mathew 10:14, to do if a village refused to hear their message.

And so, with a heavy heart I left this rubber plantation.

Some years later a lady came to my clinic. The child with her had a messy-looking hair lip. The little girl stood by as I listened to the mother's request. It was simple. The lady had a tumor on her back which she complained made carrying her basket from her plantings of manioc root too difficult. She asked me if I could remove the tumor. Then and there, with due preparation, I applied local anesthesia and began to remove the tumor. It was rather involved, and I had to go deeper than what I anticipated. Fortunately the tumor was benign.

When she returned so the stitches could be removed, I asked her about her little girl and the cleft lip.

"Oh, she was born that way," she replied.

"Yes, but we can fix that. When she grows up, how do you think she will feel when she looks at herself in the mirror?"

The mother consented to the surgery, which was going to cost her sixty cents for suture and anesthetic. After explaining the process to correct her mouth while she was under local anesthesia, the little one was ready.

I had developed a trick in doing cleft lips. Before surgery I prepared one of my wife's curlers. Through each little square, I slipped a strip of adhesive tape to go one way across the face and did the same on the other side of the curler. The incision was closed with gently tied sutures with the knot to the side of the incision, only to "snug up" the joining tissue. The curler adhesive was stretched across the face and applied. The result was to "purse" the mouth, thus maintaining articulation. The sutures were not tight, so when all of this was removed days later, there was almost no sign of the sutures and only a hair-line marked the incision.

When the mother saw her daughter with the new look. "Why did you do this for her?" The tone of her voice challenged me to express my mission to the people.

I remembered the rubber plantation – Jacob's Cut across from Jaguar Beach – and the grizzly old man who worshipped spirits and who had chased me away, and used the same answer. "I did this in the name of the Jesus who sent me."

"Yes, for a long time I was afraid to come here because I thought you would take vengeance on us. We would have done that to you.

"My God is compassionate," I told the dear lady, "and He whom I serve has given me His compassion for people."

A fool finds pleasure in wicked schemes,
but a person of understanding delights in wisdom.

King Solomon, in Proverbs 10:23 (NIV)

Chapter 39: PITY OR COMPASSION?

A young fellow came into my clinic with his straw hat pulled down to his ears. He was wearing a long-sleeve shirt with his collar buttoned in that tropical heat. He sat in the chair. "Can you cure me?"

"OK, let's see what we can find. Take off your hat, roll up your sleeves and unbutton your collar." When he did this, his swollen ears and nose became visible. I palpated the nodules on his arms.

"You touched me. Nobody touches me."

I asked if it hurt when I touched him. I knew he could feel little or nothing. I replied that I was trying to determine what his illness might be. I suspected a form of Hansen's disease, leprosy, which may develop in one of three forms as I understood it. The fact that I touched him greatly affected him. It showed him I was not afraid of what he had. The young fellow probably knew he had something bad because everybody shied away from him.

My goal with everyone I treated was to express compassion, win the person's trust, and treat them successfully. Often that would lead to follow up so I could discuss the next course of action with the patient.

I explained to this young fellow how to take the medication and increase the amount in regular increments over a period of weeks. I told him to stay out of the sun, eat only fish with scales, eat no turtle and no pork or reptiles. Eat plenty of fruit. Three months passed. He came back for a check-up.

When Jesus dealt with people, there were three characteristics evident in His communication. He dealt specifically with the individual: the woman at the well, the young student lawyer of

Mosaic Law, and the blind beggar, for example. Jesus always spoke with compassion and never pity. In a most gentle way, Jesus confronted people. It was the truth of His declarations that confronted the person, not his manner.

My goal has been: Be Compassionate; Be Specific; Confront in love.

"So," three months later I asked, "how are you doing?"

"I'm getting better" he declared.

"You look the same as you did three months ago. How can you tell me you're getting better?" (I confronted him in love.)

"I am getting better because I am no worse than I was the day I came here."

He was right as right could be. If this strain of leprosy had not been treated when we began therapy, the deterioration in his face and on his hands would have made him virtually unrecognizable.

Compassion! The word was out.

"When Jesus saw the multitudes (of individuals), He was moved with compassion."

BOOM!

In walked a man whose hand was a mess! He had been hunting across the river. His shotgun, still loaded, lay behind him on the canoe bench. It had no trigger guard. When he reached for the shotgun on the canoe seat behind him, he grabbed the gun by the barrel and proceeded to pull it alongside. As he did so, the trigger hit the edge of the canoe seat and—boom! Part of his hand went with it.

In quite some pain he told me his story. What to do? I got some tools ready and after cleaning him up a bit, I relieved the pain with a local anesthetic to the damaged hand and what fingers remained. I cut away some of the tissue and trimmed some bone. Pretty soon he had a functional hand and a good reminder to use a trigger guard and not carry a loaded shotgun unless in the jungles. The dear man did not need someone to give him a lesson or scold him. Compassion showed

I cared and felt as bad for him as perhaps he did that this happened, but with tender care I fixed it.

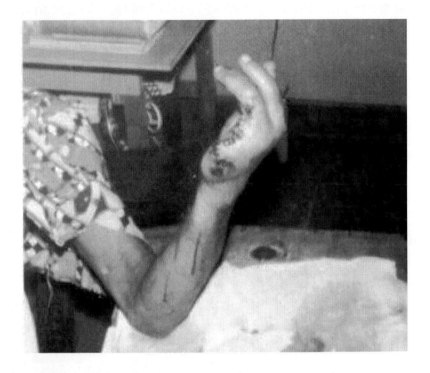

"When Jesus saw the multitudes, He was moved with compassion." I believe that Jesus looked on the individual. He looked at many and saw each one. Every life is important to God. God`s compassion is a far different value system from one of pity based on altruistic ideals.

He is the key. He makes the difference.

SEW HIM UP?

A woman came trudging up the walk to the waiting room door. I was standing there looking in the yard to see if anyone was still waiting. "Granny" had her hand on a little boy in tow who either got into a bottle of ketchup or was in a bad way. *"Doutor, pode dar um jeito nele?"* Can you patch him up? Whatever needed sewing was hidden under this mass of matted hair. What a mess. Granny carried the most distraught look one could imagine. Maybe it was worse than it looked or maybe it was not so bad.

I enlisted help and with warm water we could finally see the extent of the damage. In our Amazon world, many a tree was felled and fashioned into a square timber from which many boards were sawn. The timber was set up on a high structure, the board lines were marked, with one person above standing on the timber and the other below. The timber had been marked with a string soaked in old flashlight batteries and "snapped" to mark each line along which to saw. Rain will not smudge the line.

Granny's boy had been climbing up and down on this rig and playing tag. One of the planks slid, and as sharp as they are, clipped the scalp off his head, probably almost as well as the fabled red men of the early days of the west. And there it hung, still intact!

Poor Granny. She had no idea how serious this was, but she did what she could. She brought the boy to me.

It was a long, messy job sewing stitches and more stitches. I had to figure out where to start so that I would not have scalp left at the end of the circuit around his head. The kid was quiet as a mouse, his scalp well anesthetized. I am quite certain he was expecting a good thrashing from his father when Granny told him.

How one treats people is probably more important in the long run than the touch of the scalpel or suture. Most, like this rascal, have probably learned their lesson without being given a tongue lashing from me. At any rate, compassion is the watchword. For some it is a long way down the road of life until some moment brings a thought back to remember one who cared.

A lot of "seed" is sown for some of it to take root and produce benefit for a future generation.

For the Lord grants wisdom! His every word is a treasure of knowledge and understanding.

Proverbs 2:6 (TLB)

Chapter 40: A SCALPEL IN THE HAND

Yes, but in whose hand? This thought crossed my mind a number of times. In the same way that God used my dear wife Barbara to start me on a career as a dentist to our river people, God used her to instigate me more than once to "go at it" with the scalpel.

There on Great Snail Lake a man arrived by canoe with his son. He showed me that one of his son's eyes was closed due to a growth on the eye lid. *"O doutor pode operar o tumor?"*(Can the doctor operate on the tumor?) I was attending to teeth and everything in a little palm leaf shack.

I tried to explain to the man that my humble little clinic offered no condition to do this surgery. He replied to question if it was not my hand and scalpel that in the end would do what needed to be done. I continued to explain the gravity of this surgery.

Barbara looked at me as only a wife can do with eyes that said, *Why don't you? No one else will.* The reality of the matter was that nowhere would this man find help if I turned him away. "I'll do it." Barbara's look said, S*ee how simple it is?*

With fear and trembling, I marked off the route of the scalpel with a pen, applied the anesthetic, and went at it. The danger was great. If I cut the tear duct, the kid would have a dry eye and eventually go blind, as happens with some forms of Hansen's disease (leprosy). I had no proof as to what this tumor was, so I opted for the long, tedious use of the scalpel to extirpate it entirely, staying in healthy tissue. God's hand protected mine from touching the tear duct.

I closed the incision, taught the father how to change the dressing, and away by canoe he went.

Some years later on board a riverboat, a man greeted me. His son, quite a healthy young fellow, was traveling with him. The father asked If I remembered him. I was lost to the context. He reminded me that I had operated on his little boy. And there before me was that young man. I couldn't remember which eye I'd treated, but the son did. He hadn't a scar nor a mark.

A Distraught Father

The dear man was in misery. He desperately needed my help, yet at the same time he feared criticism and reprisal for calling on the services of one who was off limits. He told me that his teenage son had a badly swollen leg and was in agony, screaming with pain. My mental recorder did a fast backward until I was visualizing a surgical suite during my studies. A young man was brought in from Hollywood with an indescribable swollen leg due to infection.

Now, here in the middle of nowhere, I feared seeing this teen. When I got to the house, he was thrashing around in desperation. My instruments were ready. A scalpel was the key. I asked the father for newspaper or whatever he had that in a minute or two would be incinerated and destroyed.

When we were ready, I instructed the teen to lie still for the next minute or two right where he lay on the bare wood floor. The maneuver would have to be without local anesthetic, and there was no way I could put him to sleep and yet do the procedure that would last a second or two. Sheets of paper were placed under his leg and on the plain wood floor.

I instructed the father to hold the boy's feet and turn his face away. The boy agreed to hold his hands locked over his chest. I located the scalpel just above his knee and along the side where the ugly swelling was most apparent. With one swift and deep stroke, I ran the scalpel up his thigh. There was an explosion of material from the incision. By the time the boy screamed, it was all over. After cleaning up the mess and caring for the wound, which needed to remain un-sutured at present, a long course of medication would follow. Before I left, the teen was asleep there on the floor, resting in the arms of relief.

Marbles?

A lady who attended the preaching services at the little church on the river bluff, kept after me, week after week. Her face looked as if she had some marbles stuffed under the skin. Couldn't I take them out? Finally I said I would. We set the date and she arrived.

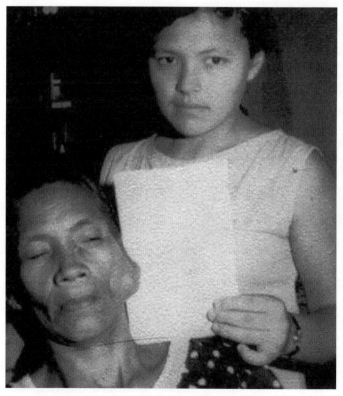

After everything was ready, I applied a local anesthetic. I made an incision just anterior of the carotid artery by her ear and ran along under the arch of her jaw to beneath her chin. It was a tedious process to open a flap and work around the three branches of the facial nerve.

I had to avoid facial paralysis. After two hours under local anesthetic, I placed a drain and closed up with a fine suture. Days later I removed the drain and found no infection.

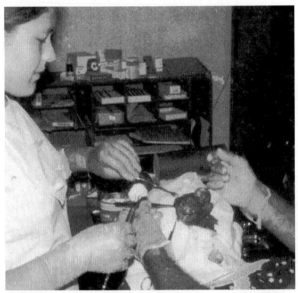

Rute, daughter of a deacon in the church, learned a few skills to assist "Dr. Luis."

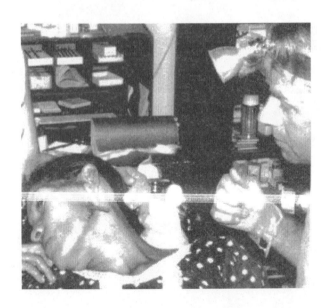

The surgery appeared to have taken a few years off her face. When the blade began its travel along the skin, one could never imagine the end result.

The Note Didn't Say

"Pastor, please attend to this lady" was all the note said. The lady brought the note to me as I was sawing pieces of wood for Vacation Bible School. The kids would be nailing the pieces together to make a clothes rack for their house. In most cases, clothes were just piled on something. I was covered with sawdust which clings well to perspiration.

When she handed me the note, I recognized that it had been written by a school teacher who lived about a day downriver. I asked the lady if she wanted me to go on board the boat to see the person. I still didn't understand whom the treatment was for.

"No, I'll bring him here," she replied. I was finishing the wood cutting for the Vacation Bible School when the lady came around the corner carrying in her arms someone covered with a sheet. I lifted the sheet. The odor was overpowering. The most pathetic little guy, eight or nine years old, looked up at me. He was burned from head to toe. They had come from a day and a half down the Mataurá River from where they lived and then turned up the Madeira to Manicoré.

As I showered and changed, I could not bring myself to decide on a first step. Barbara was with me. The only place not subject to burns was his little bottom as he had on a very tight pair of shorts.

As the story unfolded, the little guy was quite a rascal. He had been bouncing in the hammock, which stretched across the room of this palm house where everybody sat around talking, mending a net, or whatever. On a post over the hammock was a little shelf with a *lamparina* that shone throughout the room. This open wick kerosene lamp was standard in most river dwellings. With his wild bouncing, the lamparina slid off the shelf and landed on him in the hammock. Mother should have wrapped him in the cloth hammock to smother the flame. Rather, she grabbed a towel and tried to put out the flame. She had no knowledge that a kerosene-fed fire is extinguished differently from one of paper or wood.

Barbara held the little guy by his bottom with her arm propped on her knee. I poured a surgical type liquid soap, diluted in water, all over his body. We placed him on the only bed in a room for which I had affixed a screen on the window. The choice I made for therapy was to *not* mess with the burn. We kept him in as clean an environment as was possible. We taught his mother how to feed and care for him.

About two weeks passed. The rumor was that I had mummified the kid, because no one could live with that much of the body burned. And how tongues wag! One day a group of ladies stopped in the yard and asked if they could see the boy's body. The implication "see the body" implied the mummified body of the kid.

"Please look through the screen, but don't talk to him too much, or he may become too excited." Did those women ever give me a funny look!

When the burn shells fell off, they did so in a mysterious way. The boy's skin looked like that of a new-born. He had one little reminder on his chin that left a slight scar.

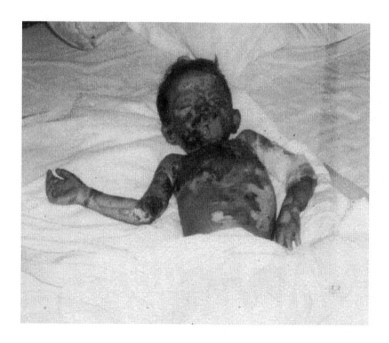

A "Present" From His Honor the Mayor

I was sitting at my desk in what I chose to call my "clinic" trying to sort out some of the mess on my desk that always got postponed till later. No one was in the waiting room.

"Hey, I've got something for you." It was the mayor's voice.

"Come on in," I replied.

He brought me a boy, about twelve years old, who had a barbed steel spear-head across and through his throat. It would have been on the end of a long arrow for spearing fish. The arrow had been broken

off, and the barbed spear remained and had a protrusion where it had
been connected to the shaft.

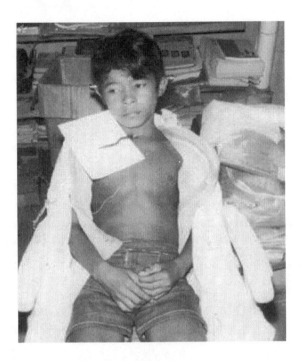

A closer examination revealed that the point of the spear was doing a
tap dance on the carotid artery in his neck. To attempt to push the
spear on through would rupture the artery. Death was that close. To
retract the spear, full of a multitude of barbs that had been created in
the making of the spear, was thought to be an impossibility that would
rip tissue to shreds in his neck. In the end, it would give the mayor
good grounds to avenge himself on the Evangelical "doctor." I prayed
for God's touch. *When there is no out, never say never*, I thought.

I began to turn the spear on its own axis, maintaining a slight
negative pressure. The boy was very calm and accepted his
predicament. Two boys in a canoe, each with his own bow and arrow,
had been spearing fish along the shallows of the river. When one boy
swung his bow and arrow on the moving fish, the other boy's neck
came into line as he released his arrow. Had the arrow not been as

large a diameter as it was, the spear and arrow may have traveled further though the boy's neck.

I continued to turn the spear in the boy's neck on its own axis. To me, the result was miraculous. The barbs evidently filled with soft tissue and the spear began coming out the same route as it took entering his neck. The carotid artery was safe from danger. The boy, too, was free from the spear. The boy rather stoically thanked me and was gone. No infection or untoward reaction occurred. The mayor seemed to think that there was nothing to it and left.

Yes, a scalpel in the hand, but in whose hand?

I thought again of the old violin put up at an auction. Nobody wanted to bid on it. An elderly man walked to the front and asked to touch the violin. He tuned it a bit and began to play. Evidently he had the touch of a master. The violin almost talked. Bids started and climbed. A person could think the violin knew the touch of the master's hand.

Our Lord brings that touch on what is done in His name.

And if God cares so wonderfully for flowers that are here today and gone tomorrow, won't he more surely care for you, O men of little faith?

Matthew 6:30 (TLB)

Chapter 41: NO PLACE TO HIDE

Feeling relief that I was all caught up with things, I took a walk along the path on the edge of the bluff as I headed for the river port in our village. As I looked up, two men coming towards me were carrying a third man in a chair, a spattering of blood leaving a trail.

The man in the chair was the motorman on a riverboat. The captain had been maneuvering to tie up in the port. He complained to the motorman that he was not getting enough power out of the engine to pull in against the river current, which was quite strong near the port.

Leaving the engine running in neutral, the motorman dove over the side in order to remove any weeds that might have been clogged in the giant propeller. The captain became impatient and feared his riverboat would drift onto the shoals. Unable to locate the motorman, not knowing that he dived under the boat to free the weeds, the captain pushed the huge lever on the engine into Forward.

At that precise moment the motorman, who had just freed the propeller from the weeds, came to the surface. One turn of the propeller clipped and cut into his Achilles tendon on the back of his ankle and with a snap like a sling-shot, the tendon retracted up his leg.

The two men carrying the man in the chair brought him to where we could place him on a table and stop the bleeding. With an instrument I reached inside the calf of his leg and attached a number of strands of silk suture to the tendon and began traction to pull the tendon back down to his heel.

I dripped with perspiration, partly from the strain as well as the intense heat. Eventually I was able to tie the tendon to the cartilage on the heel with stainless steel sutures and closed the incision. I wrote up a description of the procedure and recommended to the motorman that he be examined by a surgeon in the capital city of Manaus, where the riverboat would eventually arrive many days later to off-load the products collected up and downriver.

Almost two months later, passing by the port in my outboard, I recognized the river trader's boat of that episode. I zipped around, tied up alongside and climbed on board.

"Where's the guy who clipped his Achilles tendon on the prop?"

"There he is carrying that crate along the deck," was the reply.

I greeted the man. "How's your leg? What did the surgeon in Manaus do for you?"

"I didn't go to a doctor. I feel fine. No limp, no pain, no anything!"

I stood there on the deck of the river trader's boat, astounded at his answer.

I couldn't believe it. He never had any infection, no swelling – nothing!

I am very certain that it was the touch of God's good hand upon me. God does what He chooses to do because it honors Him. The touch of the Master's hand, that's it!

"Sing to him, sing praise to him;
tell of all his wonderful acts."

King David 1 Chronicles 16:9 (NIV)

"In Him we live and move and have our being."

St. Paul in Athens, Greece, in Acts 17:28 (NIV)

Chapter 42: HAVE CLINIC, WILL TRAVEL

Along rivers and lakes of the Madeira River, there were days when I extracted up to seventy or eighty teeth. When my older children, Beth or David, came along, they kept a count.

In most instances, everyone needing attention would gather in the one large room of the plantation. The main room was covered with palm leaf thatch and a rough-hewn wood floor. A board served as a bench fixed against the palm walls on either side of the room. A small table would be placed in the middle of the room which served to hold my instruments. A basin of water, laundry soap and towel completed the layout. Part of my kit was one of Barbara's cookie sheets on which I could flame my instruments with a squirt of alcohol.

I arranged the room so that those needing teeth extracted sat on one side and those to consult sat on the opposite side. I began by giving a nerve block to three or four mouths, depending on how many teeth would come out of each mouth. While doing this, I was listening to the others discussing their illnesses with each other. There was much to hear. When I examined the person, I might question concerning something I overhead them talking about among themselves, about things which they might forgot to mention to me. There was no privacy because everyone heard each other's story of their illness. It was a good situation in which to talk about hygiene germs, worms and whatever. It was the way things were normally done in the culture of the region.

At some moment a lady would bring me some food. It usually consisted of a bowl with some cooked roots and fish from the river or game hunted from the jungle. A little dish with coarse salt, very hot peppers, a liter bottle of brown water from the river and a gourd full of manioc meal rounded out the menu. Everybody watched me eat. Most jungle folk ate with a spoon that was packed by their thumb with a mix of manioc meal and the food, which was very simple and tasty. After eating, I would complement the lady who prepared the food about it being so delicious.

"Do you like that kind of monkey?" I was asked "Do you prefer wild boar roasted or in the pot? How do you enjoy wild turkey?"

When it came to talking about fish, I knew many by name. Each "delicacy" had its own unique preparation. Occasionally I was treated to turtle or some other reptile.

I returned to taking care of these dear people. They seemed to me to be very passive and stoic (without hope?) when dealing with their illnesses and treatment of them.

One village I stopped at consisted of fifteen or so palm houses in a bend of a small river. When I turned off the motor, I could hear a great deal of coughing. An elderly man squatted on his haunches, as is their custom, up there on the river bluff. The cough sounded like one of the monkeys found in the jungle with a large head and a leathery sheath of skin from its throat to his chest. The noise that monkey makes sounds like a person growling from deep in the throat. The monkey is called the Guariba (gwah-reeba). Locally we called it the Zog-Zog. It makes a racket that can be heard for long distances through the trees.

Some of the people had whooping cough, which is really life-threatening to those who have not received a vaccination. In those remote regions no one had access to vaccinations or even knew that there was such a thing. "Is the cough bad?" I asked.

"No, so far only ten have died." They redefined stoicism.

I believe most of those whom I treated at the rubber plantations and along the rivers and lakes were drawn by hope. A by-word often heard was, "This man cares." When you have compassion for their suffering, you give away part of yourself each time. To serve the sick and heal in Jesus' name is an honor. So many hung on to the hope of healing and would wait quietly and patiently for their turn. It became known that "he turns none aside and only stops after he has seen everybody." I often drove the boat home totally drained of energy or simply hung my hammock and mosquito net at the plantation where I was, to be on my way by dawn.

The Good Samaritan of St. Luke's chapter ten was different from the murderous robbers who stole from the man leaving him beaten, more dead than alive. The Good Samaritan was different from the religious leaders of that day. They had no time for others. The Good Samaritan saw the man half dead; had compassion on him; stopped to care for him, went out of his way to take the dear man for further care. By his actions the Good Samaritan was saying, *"What's mine is yours. I care about you."*

Jesus told this parable to show that we go through life believing in some coin we live by; a value system which, whatever it be, motivates us in one way or another.

"What's yours is mine," say the takers.

"What's yours is yours and what's mine is mine," say the keepers.

The Good Samaritan says, "What's mine is yours."

And your coin of life is …?

Love which requires a reciprocal response is *not* love.

Love just gives and gives.

Jesus replied, "Love the Lord your God with all your heart and with all your soul and with all your mind.' This is the first and greatest commandment.

Matthew 22:37-38 (NIV)

Chapter 43: "THE WATERFALL OF THE TWENTY-TWO" AND A PLANE FLIGHT HOME

I was on board a local airline flying home from Manaus to Humaitá. The twin engine DC-3 took about two and half hours for this flight. The only navigational aid was a radio beacon, when it worked, situated upriver, to the South at Porto Velho. Often as not it was off the air. Our DC 3 hit some rain and heavy cloud cover so the plane bounced about quite a bit in turbulence.

I looked at my watch and thought, *That's strange. We're about twenty-five minutes overdue.* I was sitting forward near the cabin door. Just then the door opened and out stepped one of the two pilots. He looked very disconcerted. He was dripping with perspiration.

"Are we about to arrive in Humaitá?" I asked.

"Do you live there?"

"Yes, I do."

"Come here" he ordered.

I followed him into the cabin. He shut the door. "Where are we? We're lost!"

I peered out at a mass of clouds everywhere. No radio beacon beamed through the jungle. Just then a hole opened in a cloud and right below was the "Waterfall of the Twenty-two." I knew the place.

Years back a boat load of rubber hunters were headed down a river they did not know. Their big boat went with the current, only needing to be steered. From upriver no one hears a waterfall until they are too close. The boat, twenty-two men, and all their crude rubber spilled over these high falls. A long time later huge balls of crude rubber and pieces of a large boat and oars floated downriver. All twenty-two lives were lost.

"That's the Falls of the Twenty-two," I exclaimed.

Immediately they wanted to know, "Which way is Humaitá from here?" I suggested a point on the compass. They did a tight banking turn and began to slow their engines and reduce altitude. When we landed, they taxied off the hard clay air strip and the engines quit. We were safe and sound on the ground. No better place to run out of fuel with an airplane. The God who is there *was* there. There's no such thing as luck.

A FALL OF WATER?

Protection came in many forms. I had gone downriver and into a winding creek-like waterway called an *igarapé* which connected a lake in the jungle to the outside river world. Six months of the year the rising Madeira River fed its waters into the lake which rose throughout the rainy season. The floating plants, fish and wildlife moved through and along this waterway.

From the end of the rainy season and through the dry season, the cycle reverses, and the water flows out of the lake towards the river. This waterway kept adjusting its path over the years as trees along its course fell into it and forced the current to cut a new path around or through. The ever present loops in the course of flow often gave longer waterways a serpentine look from the air as a result. The old Swedish-made Arquimedes outboard was a two opposing-cylinder engine. It was so old that it started by winding a cord around the fly wheel each time one pulled, until the engine finally started.

I was in the lake ministering for some days. The slowly falling lake level left through this waterway I was going through to get back to the Madeira. I was not aware how fast the water level in the waterway was dropping as it ran out to the Madeira at the end of the dry season. The outflow ended where it spilled into the Madeira River.

The outboard rumbled along down the waterway. The closer I got to the river, the faster the water moved. Soon I realized that I was in a V-type trough of tree trunks that seemed to rise higher on both sides. The effect of the shape of the mass of fallen trees caused my little wooden boat to drop ever lower within this canyon of tangled tree trunks that had in some earlier time flopped into the water to form a massive wall on both sides. I stopped the outboard and tipped it up to get the prop and lower part out of the water. From then on, just my canoe paddle would steer me along. Faster and faster my boat moved. This was crazy! I knew the river was close by the looks of the forest. All of a sudden I was swept around a curve to look out at a riverboat tied up at the mouth of the waterway where it met the river. Something looked funny. The men on deck were watching me approach, but they appeared to be below me. All of a sudden my boat and I shot out into space. About five feet below, I hit the surface of the river. I had been sitting toward the stern of my boat and with the weight of the motor, we went out the chute!

The men on the deck of the riverboat just looked without a word as I paddled up to them. "You didn't just come out of there did you?"

If they only knew who was watching over me. The God who is there, was there!

But the eyes of the LORD are on those who fear him, on those whose hope is in his unfailing love.

Psalm 33:18 (NIV)

Chapter 44: ONE HAND WASHES THE OTHER

There was a tightrope to walk in many circumstances that I found myself. It was often fraught with overtones of power or politics. Teaching night classes at the local school was not something I needed to fill up my time in this jungle village. When I got home from classes about 10 pm, I still had some lab work to do for returning patients the following morning.

Teaching was, however, an opportunity for others to "read" my life. After all, had not God given me the privilege to be His light? One hope I had was to teach the Biblical point of view of man as part of the religion curriculum in the school.

I was sitting in the teacher's lounge. Enter the judge. In this secondary school there was a class period for religion. It was taught by a priest whom I knew. Person to person, we got along well in the community. We worked together in a government effort to alphabetize the people. MOBRAL–MOvement BRAzilian to ALphabetize. Of sixty-six groups in our municipality (we would say "county"), my responsibility was for the ones along the river. The priest was responsible for the ones in the village. We had "volunteered" for this government effort. He wouldn't serve if I wouldn't.

In the school, a few of the students were young people from our church. Along with my classes, teaching science and other subjects to the teachers-to-be. I was approached by an assortment of students to teach religion giving students an option to either attend our class or that of the priest, "Padre Ricardo."

In the teachers' lounge, I struck up a conversation with our municipal judge who also taught in the school. He opened the dialogue by asking, "Professor, is there any way in which we can assist you in your responsibility as a teacher?"

I ventured to propose the idea of teaching an elective in religion. His prompt reply was very smooth.

"Fine," he said, "When you have as many of your religion as Padre Ricardo has of his, then we can consider the possibility. After all, Brazil is a democracy."

"Oh your excellence, "I replied, "I rather thought that in a democracy any minority should have the same privilege as anyone else."

Well, he stuttered a bit and said we could talk again on another occasion. I sensed that this was a dodge.

I glanced up at a rather high shelf in the lounge. "Look at those beautiful books. Do they belong to the school?"

He looked up and conceded to me that I could give them to my science class students. That shelf in the lounge held about two dozen New Testaments with the Imprimatur of the Roman Catholic Church. He didn't know what they were. They were gold lettered, hard cover editions. In that I had a large group of nuns in a class on general science, I gave each one a present of this New Testament.

In geology, I was teaching how great earthquakes, volcanic eruptions and other upsets may increase as the time for Christ's return comes nearer. I pointed out where to read about this in Matthew's Gospel. So, the judge did me a good turn. It cost him nothing, but the new Testaments were distributed on his authority.

I later learned that our friend the judge had an "investment" in a brothel just outside the village. The bishop had told the judge that if he made any concessions to this pastor/professor, that he, the bishop, would "blow the lid off" the judge's brothel. The price of silence by the bishop was conditioned on suppressing any pro-active effort to favor the pastor in the education of the youth. I had been this route with a wedding in Humaitá. The "mail" was very "black" and had nothing to do with the postal system.

A phrase in our culture said, "One hand washes the other." It often meant one underhanded favor was repaid with another underhanded favor. To which I usually replied with a jovial smile to ease the confrontation, "Yes, unless one hand dirties the other."

Salt irritates. Light hurts the eyes. Jesus told us "Be wise as serpents and harmless as doves."

When the director of the High School handed me a check for the period of teaching, I endorsed the check to the mission account in Manaus and asked her to deposit it on her next trip there.

She looked at the check and back to me. "Pretty slick! You make it look like the mission will get the money, but you probably have power over that account."

"*Dona*, don't judge others by the way you manage your affairs."

A rather sickly smile crossed her face. She would find out at the bank in Manaus that I did not have signature on the mission bank account. Only the mission Field Treasurer had that authority.

In the end she gained great respect as she learned that I would not wash one hand with another, thereby getting mine dirty.

Jesus said,

*"Let your light so shine before men that they can see your good works
and glorify your Father in heaven."*

Matthew 5:16 (KJV)

Chapter 45: PUSH THE ENVELOPE?

Life moves on. After the many years along the river, we moved to Manaus for a number of reasons to do with our commitment to the mission and to accommodate our kids in Brazilian schools, not available in the interior in the villages where we had lived. Part of my responsibility was to act on behalf of the mission before the Brazilian government. I received the incumbency to negotiate the importation of a float plane to expedite time that otherwise be consumed in long river trips.

Diplomacy when dealing with the government suggests a rule of thumb to always avoid pressing an issue that may receive a *no*. Pushing the envelope can end in refusal.

In our city of Manaus, in the State of Amazonas, I was talking to the Federal Tax Bureau Office responsible for importation. Our mission had received an airplane on floats for ministry in the Amazon region. I stood in front of the desk of the Director of Importation. He did not invite me to sit down. This was the first negative signal. It meant "Don't bother me."

I tried to convince him of the use and of the importance of the airplane to serve the river people. My appeal and reasoning seemed to produce no softening of his attitude. If I were to push the envelope any harder, I'd get a firm *no*, and that would mean I could never again make an appeal for the float plane's importation.

I looked at my watch and made an obvious expression of surprise. "Look at the time! I beg your leave, as I need to pick up my kids who study at the Federal Technical High School."

"Oh, your kids study at the Federal High School?" He replied with equal surprise. "Mine do, too." Interpretation: he thought that because I was from another country, my children would study in a school for foreigners. The director visibly changed in his attitude.

I inquired if I could return and hear any instructions that he might give for the importation of the plane. Frankly, I was convinced he was going to say no or send me on a paper trail chase that could go on for months.

A new player came into the room, the director's assistant who did all the leg work for this department. As I turned to leave the room, I faced the assistant, who had arrived at the desk behind me moments before. He had recognized my voice. "Oh, Pastor, how are you?"

Before I could respond he turned to his boss, the Director, and blurted out, "This man saved my son's life." His son, an engineer on the Trans Amazon Highway, was now one of the key persons in the National Highway Department in the Federal Capital of Brasilia.

The story was quite embellished as the father told it to his boss. I went back in my memory to those long nights in the jungle village. I had been called to the residence of the road building company. A man who seemed to be in a quite desperate state of emotion met me. "My son is very sick with a high fever. He will not let anybody near him, but he trusts you."

I went into the room where his son lay in bed in a rather disquieting state of affairs. After examining him, it was clear that he had tertian malaria caused by the Falciparum strain. I had seen so much of this fever that blood work was not needed for the diagnosis. The young road engineer was in bad shape partly due to procrastinating to accept therapy or, he feared, misguided therapy. The greatest disadvantage was his fear of being sick. The first step was to gain his trust and confidence so I could proceed with what I deemed to be a rather radical treatment. Fear itself is destructive.

He finally showed a favorable consideration of the therapy I outlined to him. I stayed with him. Through the night I gave him intravenous feedings and used an anti-malarial medication on a prescribed timeline. After about thirty-six hours of constant care, he responded with improvement. In a sense, we were "out of the woods."

Now, way down the road of life, I am in this Federal Tax Office listening to the father of the highway engineer. He tells a rather dramatic account of "saving his son's life" from this life threatening bout with malaria. True it was that some of the road crew people did succumb to cerebral malaria. Their graves added to the cemetery population of Humaitá.

So who pushes the envelope? Not me! God used something that touched the heart of those empowered to make the decisions in a way only God could accomplish.

As I stepped to the door of the tax office, the director said, "Pastor, why don't you come back tomorrow. I'll put you in touch with the person who can walk you through the paper work."

The next day I returned and was summarily directed to the desk of a subordinate who already had all the papers in hand. After a brief interview, the papers were handed to me with all the rubber stamps and signatures. "And now what do I do?" I asked.

"That's it. One of our men will inspect the floatplane and will clear it."

I drove the inspector out to the cove in the river where the plane was anchored. I suggested getting a canoe to paddle out to look inside the plane, check papers, or whatever it would take for him to approve it.

"It all looks okay," he said. "Take me back to the office."

If we push the envelope, it doesn't work. But when God intervenes, just watch!

...because the gracious hand of my God was on me...

The wall builder, Nehemiah 2:8 (NIV)

Chapter 46: THE THREAD OF RADIO

A thread runs through many of the stories that were part of our experiences. And so the thread of radio weaves its way into some of the stories I relate. Our friend, Horst Marquardt of ERF Germany, Evangeliums-Rundfunk (The Evangel by Radio), brought a God-given vision to Brazil to reach the many German-speaking colonies here by radio. Some groups had migrated from Germany as far back as the time of Kaiser Wilhelm. Others came around the time of the Great War which spread over Europe. Many more came as late as World War II. Most were hard working farmers. Many were very capable manufacturers. The populations of the southern regions of Brazil were from other nations too—Russians, Poles, and Italians. A tremendous population of Japanese arrived in the early days of 1900 to work the coffee plantations.

The predominant population came from many places in Germany. In Brazil these colonies had their own newspapers, radio stations, schools and churches all in the German language or recognizable dialects.

By the beginning of World War II, Brazil was under the thumb of a dictator by the name of Getulio Vargas. He feared the influence of the German colonies might be sympathetic to the Third Reich ideology. (Far from it!). He questioned why these masses of people had migrated to a new and unknown land. Getulio Vargas decreed the end of all use of German language schools, newspapers, radio and other means of communication within the colonies. This dictator eventually shot himself, but the laws had been put into place. They were not so well enforced, but changes were eventually felt by these German speaking colonies.

On a visit to Brazil, Horst Marquardt of ERF, Wetzlar, Germany, quickly grasped the situation of these colonies and God set out to use Horst to challenge followers of Christ in Brazil to take a courageous lead. Many of those whom ERF challenged were themselves in some way connected to the colony culture and had use of the German language as well as Brazil's Portuguese language.

Edmund Spieker, who migrated from Germany to Brazil as an adolescent, took up the challenge and rallied men and women to put feet to the vision which Horst of ERF had brought from the Lord. Soon a production studio was installed in the German Baptist Church in São Paulo. As the work grew, studios moved to the adapted house of one of the church members. By 1967, a building began to rise in the city of São Paulo, to become the studios and offices of Radio Trans Mundial.

The vision grew to reach all Brazil by radio. Programs in German as well as Portuguese were broadcasting from half million watt Trans World Radio transmitters on the Island of Bonaire in the Caribbean Sea. German language programs were sent to Portuguese language radio stations, who gladly broadcast them in the regions of the colonies. Listener response was overwhelming.

God reached into the lives of many. Present generations are grandchildren of immigrant families and have become part of Brazil's culture and language. As a result of that seed planted by ERF and joined by Trans World Radio, Trans Mundial Brazil today broadcasts by satellite, over local stations, via short wave transmitters and by Internet and other electronic media, twenty-four hours a day. Programs are also aired in indigenous languages to the vast regions of the Amazon. We had the privilege of carrying this vision along for the years we were directing RTM Brazil, following Edmund Spieker.

Spanish language programs were being produced in many places. After Brazil, God challenged us to help develop this radio ministry in a number of Spanish-speaking countries of Latin America and the

Caribbean. Eventually we would have the heavy responsibility of training radio producers on five continents in liaison with Trans World Radio Europe and Evangeliums-Rundfunk.

Radio stands alone where there is no person on location to communicate Jesus' words of forgiveness for sin and the promise of eternal life. And where there are any who speak and are present among the people, the radio message reinforces what that person proclaims.

Very often the radio message of the Gospel has prepared people so well with the teachings of God's book, that when the messenger of God's word appears among these people, they are ready to declare their trust in Jesus as Savior and Lord. Congregations may soon come into existence. And so the role of radio can stand alone, or it can work in cooperation with the messenger on the ground. How many places we visited in the Amazon where the radio had prepared so many to better understand what God says in His Book!

The LORD's word is flawless.

The Prophet Samuel, in 2 Samuel 22:31 (NIV)

Chapter 47: A MAN CALLED WALTER

Walter Wilke was born into one of the many farm colonies of German-speaking immigrants in the South of Brazil. He grew up in a rural community in the 1950's.

In his colony, the entire school curriculum was taught in the German Language. He married a young lady from the same language, cultural heritage and region in the early 60's. Walter and Nair were both very religious and regularly attended the church denomination of their upbringing. But God was always far away.

Then things changed. They began to listen to the German language radio programs produced by Evangeliums Rundfunk in Germany and broadcast by TWR from the island of Bonaire, in the Caribbean. Something started to happen to this young couple. Day after day they plowed and cultivated their land with their pairs of oxen. Walter and his wife each had a pair. Farm girls in the colony could handle a plow or animals as well as the men.

Early each dawn and again in the evening, Walter and his wife listened to ERF radio programs in their mother tongue. In church and elsewhere, one presumed that you did your best to be "good people," but the message they heard said something more. They learned of God's love and His forgiveness. They understood God's provision of salvation even for people whom everyone thinks are such good people.

Walter and Nair learned that God did for them what they could never do for themselves. One day Walter and his wife were upon a hilly slope plowing, each with their own pair of oxen. It happened. They tied their oxen in the shade to sit together for a rest. Walter talked with his wife Nair about the words from God they were hearing by radio and what they meant.

There in the field on the hillside, Walter and Nair knelt in prayer and asked God's forgiveness for their sinfulness and trusted in Jesus as their Savior.

To their consternation, crops began to fail and they fell on hard times. But God was at work. Walter was asked to take a job in an electrical shop. It meant a ride of nine kilometers each way on horseback from the colony to the little village. He learned much about electricity. As the world of electronics developed, Walter moved with his wife to this village. The years passed and his studious mind learned all he could. Soon the local radio station in that town contracted his services to maintain the transmitter and related equipment.

Another radio station requested his services. His abilities improved and his reputation followed him. The second station offered him three minutes a day of air time as part of his pay. Walter accepted the challenge, producing a compact three minute talk of the style with which farm people in those colonies identified. Very many times the producer of the thirty minute program that followed Walter's three minutes failed to show up at the radio studio. Everything was done live on-air in those days. Walter stepped into the thirty minute slot and just went on talking about the One who changed his life. He had only one record which he played as judiciously as possible.

During this same time that God was changing Walter's life, I was directing RTM Brazil. In the early 80's, a man came to my office at Radio Trans Mundial in the city of São Paulo. He shared his burden to do radio in a region of Brazil. I spent time giving Pastor Ivan Nunes some basic information about building a short wave radio station, towers, transmitters, and associated equipment.

Pastor Ivan started a short wave radio station but was fraught with technical problems. It was then that God led in such a way that Walter came to the rescue of this radio station. It became too much for this group to manage as they wished to produce their own programs.

Pastor Ivan eventually saw the great potential of short wave radio in Brazil. By this time Bonaire was forced to terminate its many years of short wave broadcasts. Refurbishment of antennas and transmitters on Bonaire would be a task of monumental proportions. At the same time God brought Walter into the picture. Pastor Ivan came back to talk to us at Radio Trans Mundial, the trusted name in Brazil's history of reaching people by radio, and asked RTM to take over the ministry.

As of 21 November, 2004, at the transmitter park just outside the city of Santa Maria, in the state of Rio Grande do Sul, sits a group of three short wave transmitters in testimony to God's good hand upon His work. Faithful to call His servants, God is doing it. The transmitters are linked to the twenty-four hour satellite service of RTM from production studios in São Paulo. They also offered open channel feeds to any AM or FM station in Brazil who wished to air any of the programs telling Brazil's world of redemption in Jesus Christ.

The government engineer was sent to inspect and approve the licenses or close down the operation. He told the Director of Radio Trans Mundial, "In all my years of engineering, I have never seen such a perfect installation of radio transmitters as this man Walter has constructed.

God began the radio ministry of Evangeliums Rund-Funk whose German language programs reached the ears and hearts of Walter and Nair And so God prepared a simple German colony farmer to be God's special voice to build the very best transmitters and antennas to broadcast the message of Salvation.

If the ERF programs had not been on the air for Walter to hear, would any of this have come into existence? These pieces of the puzzle we will learn more about in eternity.

...for it is God who is at work in you,
both to will and to work for His good pleasure.

Paul to those in Filipos, Greece, Philippians 2:13 (NASB)

Chapter 48: MY LOVE, THEY'VE COME!

Three students from another region of Brazil came to a rather remote region of southern Amazonas during their school vacation. They wanted to talk to people about the gospel message. "We want to reach people with the good news of the Gospel message." They trekked down a path far from the nearest dirt road. Along the trail, they stopped at sparse dwellings to talk with people. Many that they met couldn't read or write. Some would be able to read the literature they left.

They were tired, and they couldn't see any more dwellings down the long stretch of jungle trail. They asked themselves, "Should we go back? Go on?" A consensus was taken by the three, and onward they pressed.

Suddenly, they found themselves standing at the edge of a large clearing of land full of tree stumps, land soon to be planted. Palm-roofed, rough board houses sat around the forest clearing. At the nearest house, they clapped their hands to announce their arrival, standing a distance from the door. The bottom half of the door was closed to keep the pigs, chickens and ducks out of the humble abode.

A lady came to the door. "Yes, what is it?"

One of the three replied, "We don't want anything, but we are here to tell you about the one God and His son who was sent to earth to bring us salvation and forgiveness from sin…"

Before the student could finish, the woman extended her hand. "Wait a minute!"

She turned to someone in the room. "My love, they've come!"

Each of the young men looked curiously at the others. Had they been expected? Promptly, they were invited into the house and sat on rough-hewn wooden benches. Curious, they ventured a question. "What did you say to your husband?"

Her reply surprised her visitors.

"For about two years we have been listening to a radio program in Portuguese over Trans World Radio. We heard about God, His Son and His book. We have been praying to this one true God to send someone to tell us more about Him. And now He has sent you!"

They hadn't been sent to the woman and her husband only. The three soon learned that families in the jungle are staircases of kids. One in the womb, one on the breast, another hanging onto mommy's skirt, and so up they go in age. The woman sent two of her sons to gather the neighbors. One boy ran to the nearest neighbor and the other was sent over a jungle trail in the opposite direction. Each household, in turn, carried the invitation along to the next house.

At nightfall, yellow lights from open-wick kerosene lamps began to arrive from many directions. As the young folk talked to the group, they realized radio programs had provided a solid basis for understanding God's book. The teaching went on for several evenings. Evangelism and discipleship was their two-pronged effort.

Before the students departed several days later, God's spirit worked in the hearts of many who professed repentance for their sinfulness and trusted Christ for eternal salvation.

Eventually, the people sawed rough planks from the trees to build a house of worship. A circuit preacher came once a month. They started looking for a more permanent form of ministry to the growing flock. A church group was established. This story has no end!

On one occasion when I was in this region of the Amazon, I visited the little church that was started by the three visitors. I arrived at that location by a Volkswagon mini-bus that weaved in and out and around those same many tree stumps. The church was painted (a rarity), complete with windows and lighted with pressure lamps. The place was packed. I entered through a window near the pulpit.

If we could only see beyond today as God does see.

For the word of the LORD is right and true;
he is faithful in all he does.

Psalm 33:4 (NIV)

Chapter 49: ONE MOUTH — MANY EARS

If ORALITY is that culture that relays information "by word of
mouth," is the other side AURICULARITY? If the mouth speaks, do
the ears hear and remember? I believe they do.

River merchants I knew could not read a sentence but were
capable of remembering the trade accounts of customers along the
river and lakes. Of the many sick I consulted and to whom I prescribed
medication, the majority relied on their memory. Even so, I wrote in
block letters what I told them to do or to take. As such these people of
the Amazon represented what is termed an *oral culture*.

In the West Africa country of Guinea-Bissau lives a people
group called the Felupe. Theirs is one of the many tribal languages in
this coastal country. I spent six weeks there with our son Tim and his
family, who lived as the Felupe for seven years. Tim, a missionary and
linguistic scientist, is very capable in five or six languages.

A solar-powered FM radio station reaches all eighteen villages
over this coastal savannah. A Non-government Organization donated
the FM and disappeared. On an earlier visit I had given instruction to
the tribal element managing the solar FM. We demonstrated the use of
microphones, mixing sound, VU meter levels, and such.

On this recent visit, our son Tim was giving in-depth training in
discipleship to key leaders from several different villages. These men
were progressing well in their understanding of leadership responsi
bilities as the Lord's ambassadors to their people. Part of this training
Tim dedicated to preparation in story telling which could now be
effectively done by radio. We used Tim's laptop and a head set with

mike and earphones. We utilized a simple software program to record digitally, for reproduction.

Each man was assigned a Bible story to tell in his own words to the rest of the group. Most text is available to them in the Creole out of ancient Portuguese, but the Felupe tell the stories in their tongue. As they go from Creole to Felupe, they are acutely aware of nuances that could mean the difference between a clear portrayal of the Bible story in Felupe and the danger of what we call syncretism.

We were well along in training the story-tellers which lessons Tim was translating from my Portuguese into both Creole and Felupe. At this phase of the process, an "old friend" showed up who used to give me repeated "bouts" during the years we lived in the Amazon jungles. Yes, Falciparum Malaria knocked me out of commission. The fever and chills became so intense I could no longer function. This was a blessing after all, because it enabled Tim and the Felupe men to continue to experiment and reach a measurable proficiency in telling the stories. When they heard the recording of themselves, there was no way to hold them back. They are born story tellers. In an oral (nothing in writing) society, their memory recall is as good as any recorder.

The stories they tell on the tribal FM produce a two-fold impact. Those who are deep into their spirit worship are learning of the God who is all powerful, is ever present, and who cares. The believers learn by Bible story illustrations more about the God in whom they trust and how to follow Him more clearly. They learn of His power, protection and guidance. Non-believers learn this too.

Radio multiplies the voice of the story of Jesus and writes the words on the hearts of men. As the voice speaks, some hear with the ear, others hear with the heart.

Jesus said, "He who has ears to hear, let him hear."

The person who does the planting or watering isn't very important, but God is important because he is the one who makes things grow.

1 Corinthians 3:7 (TLB)

Chapter 50: TEACHING – A SEARCH FOR RESOURCES

When you are challenged to train a group of people for radio program production and related activities, do you tell those you teach what talents you are looking for or, do you do the looking to analyze the talents of those to whom you teach radio production?

I prefer to teach those who do not have prior bad habits. I expect my students in training to learn practical approaches to communicating. One on one is the key to what is often called mass media. One pair of ears at a time listens to the sound. It's called mass media, but radio can be the most individual means of communication short of a telephone conversation.

By invitation, I was in eastern Paraguay with the challenge to seek and hire talent for an FM radio station for which the license was already in hand. The FM would operate in three languages: Guarani, Low German, and Spanish. The course was scheduled for three days only.

I always work through the national director of Radio Trans Mundial for whatever country on any project. The radio station project manager who invited us was very skeptical that we could accomplish his goal of getting a team together to operate the FM.

I taught this course in Paraguay, in Spanish, which has some interesting nuances out of the Guarani frame of mind. I scheduled mornings for classes. I did not tell the students what I was looking for. Of the group of six, certain factors became evident. One young woman said hardly a word but wrote constantly, taking notes. A fellow in the group could hardly stop talking whenever given the chance. There was another fellow in the group who seemed very quiet and attentive to capture any little detail.

In the afternoon I suggested we take a look at the studio and experiment a bit. The talker went for the microphone. The detail guy was enchanted with the buttons on the control panel. I suggested in Spanish that we play at making up a program format. First question then was, "Which language should we use?"

"*Bueno*," I replied. "In whichever one you feel comfortable."

"We use all three with equal ease, said the mike guy.

We discussed different program formats: news, sports anecdotes for life, and reflections on Scriptures. The woman, who wrote so prodigiously, sketched out formats as quickly as I discussed them with the team. We did some exciting dry runs that day and more training the second day. We had pretty much located three of the six persons to compose a viable team for the local FM for that Paraguayan city of Caaguazú.

To the surprise of the inviter, he was beside himself with joy and greatly relieved. The license required the station to be on air several weeks hence, in Spanish, Guarani and Low German.

MORAL OF THE STORY: If those you train know what you are looking for, you will have volunteers that aim to fill a job spot rather than manifest a talent which you diagnose as to where it fits, *if* it fits.

...because the gracious hand of my God was on me...

Nehemiah 2.8b NIV

Chapter 51: A BITTER OUTLOOK

This phone-in to the talk show came from a woman as bitter as one could be. Fortunately she didn't use foul language or she would have been cut off. The theme of the talk show that night was "Do you know God loves you?"

This woman called in. She sounded very bitter as she told her tale of grief. She was aggressive. "You tell me God loves me? I don't believe a word of it. I live with my daughter, who's a single mother, and her two-year old child. My daughter forbids me to go near my grandchild. And you say God loves me? Why would God be so mean as to keep me from my granddaughter?"

The person on the talk show had real patience with this woman, but he was very frank. "Lady, if you want to know that God loves you, get on your knees and ask God to forgive you for a heart full of hate for your daughter and for many around you. Do this and you will see how God forgives, and how He will rebuild your life. If you do this, call us back and tell us what God did in your life. If you refuse to trust God to forgive, then don't bother to call back."

A number of calls were handled on the program and then "Mrs. Vinegar" called back. "Hello, I see you are calling back. Tell us what took place. Did you do what we recommended?" She then began to relate on air what transpired since her first call spewing acrimony against God and the world.

"When I hung up, I got on my knees in front of the couch. My daughter watched me dumfounded. "Mom, what are you doing?" she said.

"I told my daughter that I was going to ask God to forgive me for all my bitterness and hate for you and everyone around me. My daughter got down on her knees, and the best way we knew how, we asked God to forgive us and show us His love."

"My daughter told me how she had hoped for some change, as she couldn't go on with life the way we were always fighting. She forgave me, and as I talk to you on the radio program, I am holding my two-year-old granddaughter in my arms for the very first time. I can now say I know God loves me. He has forgiven me years of hostility and hate."

God can change water to wine, and He can change vinegar to honey.

For the word of the LORD is right and true;
he is faithful in all he does.

Psalm 33:4 (NIV

Chapter 52: A VOICE FOR SOLDIERS

Western Paraguay, near the border with Bolivia, is called the Chaco because the region is known for the thick jungle bush that is common there. In the center of this region is a radio station called "*La Voz del Chaco Paraguaio*" (The Voice of the Paraguayan Bush). The radio station is under the care of Mennonite Christians whose German-speaking grandfathers settled in this then-very-unhealthy region in 1927 and 1929. Today it is one of the most productive regions of the country of Paraguay for milk, grain, cotton, cattle, peanuts and a growing number of products. Their hospitals are the most sought after in the country.

The Voice of the Chaco broadcasts programs in a number of languages: Spanish, Guarani (the two official languages of Paraguay) Plaute (low) Deutsch, Hoch Deutsch, Lengua and Churupi. I had the privilege of serving this radio station training Indians of the two last languages. I worked through a translator from my Spanish to their languages.

When I was there, the radio station was broadcasting "Thru the Bible" in Spanish very early in the morning. At an army base where the new soldiers were being trained, the wife of the commandant listened to "Through the Bible" and was amazed at the impact the content was making in her life. She spoke to her husband about this. As the commandant of the military post he had the last word as to policy governing his management of the recruits. His wife suggested that he put the program over the loud speaker into the barracks where the new soldiers were. Her husband agreed. The program was piped into the barracks on the loud speaker system.

How many young men could hear the truth of the Bible at the beginning of their military lives? Will we ever know what changes God made in young men's lives because He reached into the life of the commandant's wife? And did the programs ever reach into the life of the commandant as well?

The Lord's promise is sure. He speaks no careless word; all he says is purest truth, like silver seven times refined.

Psalm 12:6 (TLB)

Chapter 53: THREE LESS ONE IS MORE

The mother and father were very devout, religious people. Life seemed very normal. They had one daughter, very beautiful. She was dating a young man who was into everything as a wild fellow who lived life in the fast lane.

Mother and father became very concerned for their daughter and the bad effect the young man was having on her lifestyle. Their very religious life did not give them any hope.

About this time the parents had been listening to a radio program produced by Radio Trans Mundial, Uruguay. The programs reached past their ears and went right to their hearts. It was not too long a time before both mother and father turned to the Lord Jesus to trust Him to be their Savior.

Sometime later the daughter could see the change in her mother and father and she eventually trusted in the Lord.

It became evident that the daughter could not continue her relationship with the young man. She told him that she could no longer enjoy the life they had been pursuing.

 Peace came to the home as both mother and father and daughter grew in their new faith in the Lord Jesus. One evening, they had just sat down to the evening meal and thanked God in prayer for His goodness. The doorbell rang.

"Mom, I'll go to the door." When she opened the door, there stood her ex-boyfriend. He attacked the daughter physically. "If I can't have you, nobody can," he said, and stabbed her many times, killing her as her mother and father looked on in horror.

The man was charged with murder and sent away to prison. But the story doesn't end there. The mother and father visited this murderer many times at the prison. After hearing the mother and father tell him many times of God's forgiveness, this man who killed their daughter came to trust the same Lord and Savior.

He serves his time for the crime he committed, but he knows God has forgiven him and the parents of the one he murdered also forgave him. He is more of a free person in prison than he was on the outside.

Can any other but the power of God forgive? Many lives were touched and added to God's family by the loss of the daughter.

"For my thoughts are not your thoughts, neither are your ways my ways," declares the LORD.

Isaiah 55:8

Chapter 54: THE NIGHT WATCHMEN

It was after eleven on a Friday evening. The talk show ended at midnight. This night it was an open line for call-ins from listeners. The topic on the talk show was about forgiveness. People called in with questions and comments. The calls were received off-air and passed along to the persons on the talk show. Two persons hosted it. One was a psychologist and one was a pastor.

A man who was a night watchman told his story on the air and declared he was going to take his life. He told of losing his wife to illness within the year and his ten children had just stopped getting in touch with him. He painted a touching picture of loneliness and despair. We learned later that he didn't even own a little portable radio. On his rounds of the factory, he heard voices and discovered that someone had left their portable radio on and tuned to this station. After the watchman told his story of woe, he declared that he would take his life and hung up.

Another call came in. It was desperate. "Please get a message on the air to that watchman. He's our father and we have been so busy with things that we have neglected to contact our father since our mom died."

The talk show discretely told the man that one of his sons had called and asked this man to call the station off-air to make arrangements to meet with the sons and daughters.

Soon they met with their dad. Because the pastor was involved in getting these folks together, they invited him along to their encounter. In time, all turned out quite well. The families invited the pastor to show them about God from the Bible, so one night a week the whole gang met in one of the homes for a study of the Bible.

Today the father is well cared for by his sons and daughters, and makes the rounds in their homes. They have declared themselves followers of the Lord Jesus through their study of the Bible and are active members of a vibrant church.

Because of a radio left behind in a factory tuned to that station, a desperate man poured out his heart in despair and hopelessness. God cared. The watchman found his family, and God found both the man in despair and his children.

"He will call upon me and I will answer in his anguish and I will be with him"

King David in Psalm 91:15

THE LAST CHAPTER IS YET TO BE WRTTEN

The move to our eternal home is ever closer.

The coin of life is spent so fast. Only what's done for our Lord will last.

A heritage for him: our children, grandchildren, and great-grandchildren who follow Him will do so much to share God's love in many places and languages.

Life is like a coin. You may spend it as you wish or as God guides, but you'll only spend it once.

Alan & Barbara Bachmann

abachmann@avmi.org
(in English, Portuguese, Spanish or German)

Biography

Alan and Barbara were strongly convinced after conversion to Christ in high school that God had prior claim on their lives. God guided them to study theology, linguistics, missionary medicine, dentistry and tropical diseases. They applied to a mission* requesting to be sent to the Amazon. They gladly stayed raising their five during those early years. After twenty-four years in the Amazon, God led them into radio and other modes of communication.

Alan directed the national radio ministry in Brazil known as Radio Trans Mundial, affiliated with Trans World Radio. During the next ten years at their invitation, he trained communicators in Spanish speaking countries of Latin America and the Caribbean. Alan was then asked to take on the responsibility of Global Training Coordinator on five continents to prepare key persons to become program producers in their own language.

The Bachmanns' five children and spouses, grand kids and greats serve God on four continents are fluent in three or four languages and at home in many cultures. Twenty nine serve in the fields of pastoral ministries, aviation, Bible translation, nursing, medicine, dentistry, education, engineering, global communications, administration in multi-national companies, public health, aesthetics and ecological agriculture.

Alan and Barbara Bachmann still reside in Brazil, and continue their missionary endeavors.

Made in the USA
Charleston, SC
02 February 2015